A HARROWSMITH GARDENER'S GUIDE

SHADE GARDENS

EDITED BY BRENDA COLE

FIREFLY BOOKS

A FIREFLY BOOK

First published in 1993 by Camden House Publishing
(a division of Telemedia Communications Inc.)

Third printing 1995

Cataloguing-in-Publication Data

Main entry under title:
Shade gardens

Includes index.
ISBN 0-921820-63-1

1. Gardening in the shade.
2. Shade-tolerant plants.
I. Cole, Brenda.

SB434.7.S53 1993   635.9'54   C92-095534-7

Published by
Firefly Books Ltd.
3680 Victoria Park Avenue
Willowdale, Ontario
Canada M2H 3K1

Published in the U.S. by
Firefly Books (U.S.) Inc.
P.O. Box 1338, Ellicott Station
Buffalo, New York 14205

Design by
Linda J. Menyes

Front cover photograph by
Margaret Hensel/Positive Images

Back cover photograph by
Lefever, Grushow/Grant Heilman

Color separations by
Mutual/Hadwen Imaging Technologies
Ottawa, Ontario

Printed and bound in Canada by
Friesens
Altona, Manitoba

Printed on acid-free recycled paper

Acknowledgements

Shade Gardens: A Harrowsmith Gardener's Guide represents, in its finished state, the commitment and cooperation of many individuals. They include art director Linda Menyes; artist Marta Scythes, who prepared the illustrations; editor Tracy Read; assistant editor Catherine DeLury; editorial assistant Jane Good; editorial production consultant Susan Dickinson; and associates Mary Patton, Christine Kulyk and Charlotte DuChene.

Contents

Introduction:
A Love of Shade
By Brenda Cole

Like most love affairs, this one was unsolicited. It happened by chance upon the purchase of our first Canadian home, a venture governed by what we could afford rather than what we wanted. After the excitement of moving in, we took stock and found we now owned a garden of gloom and doom. "Nothing will grow here," the Jeremiahs said. "You'll never make anything of this yard," warned helpful friends. We looked at the fine old trees, the patch of dusty grass masquerading as lawn and the few languishing sun lovers and imagined a shadowy place of cool repose, filled with soft colour and the haunting fragrance of damp earth and lush growth. We fell in love with shade and proved them all wrong. That yard, as our friends scathingly called our garden, was gradually transformed into one of the most charming shade gardens in town. Home to more than 500 different plants, it also became a favourite watering hole for our pessimistic friends, who quickly learned to appreciate the delights of a shady garden during the dog days of summer. Why, in a country where the summers are hot and sunny, is gardening in the shade so often abandoned as hopeless? It is true that many shady areas in gardens are tired, gloomy and drab, but they need not be so. A shaded area is like a precious gem: leave it lying around neglected for years, and you have a dull, drab stone; clean it up and lavish 7 on it the loving care it deserves, and presto, you have a shining jewel. Our gloom-and-doom garden was a dull gem indeed, but we knew in our hearts that it would respond to care and would eventually shine.

Getting Started

The first thing you must understand is that gardening in shade is no more difficult than gardening in sunny areas. It just calls for a slightly different approach and a little more care in choosing plants. Be-

The rich textures in the shade garden produce a memorable effect.

ginners should also note that using one's powers of observation and plain common sense is all that is needed to get started. Gardening skills and knowledge are not prerequisites: they are acquired gradually as one's interest grows. Every expert in the world started out knowing nothing.

Garden shade is difficult to define and degrees of shade impossible to pinpoint. When we speak of shade, we are really talking about the amount of light that penetrates an area. This light can be measured with a light meter, and the readings are of immense value to a photographer. These readings are totally useless to the gardener, though, because they change by the minute, and we have no standard with which to compare them. Shade is never static. It changes throughout the day as

the sun rises, moves overhead and sets; it changes with the seasons; and it can change almost instantly when clouds move across the sun. Fortunately, plants are able to cope with these shifting patterns. When we try to classify shade, the confusion gets worse. The almost dark conditions found under a stand of conifers, for instance, may be called full shade, dense shade or deep shade. The light coming through the sparse canopy of young deciduous leaves in spring might be termed light, filtered or dappled shade. Provided we realize that such classifications are loose guidelines, they do help us to sort things out and group plants within the limits of their adaptability.

In addition to the level of light, the condition of the soil affects the choice of plants. We may find hot, dry shade close to a south-facing wall or cool, damp shade by a north-facing fence on heavy clay soil. Under deep-rooted oaks, it may be moist and cool, but under shallow-rooted maples, it will be dry and cool. These distinctions may at first seem confusing, but remember our warning about observation and common sense. You don't have to have a science degree to distinguish hot, dry shade from cool, moist shade, but in order to do so, you have to get out into the garden, really look at what is there and get your hands dirty. Look hard, and think about the shade. Where does it fall, how long does it stay, how dense is it, does it stay year-round or only during summer and fall, as under deciduous trees? Look at the soil. Is it light and fluffy, caked hard and cracked or packed down solid? Grab a handful and feel the texture while examining what it looks like. Do this before you read about soils and how to improve them.

Soils

The study of soil is a complex science, but in very simple terms, soil is a mixture of three kinds of tiny particles and humus. Particles down to $1/50$ of an inch in size are sand, finer gritty grains to $1/500$ of an inch are silt, and even finer ones — smaller than

A foreground planting of Jack-in-the-pulpits among purple primulas flourishes in the sun-dappled shade created by the lush overhead deciduous-tree canopy.

$1/5000$ of an inch – are clay. Humus is the lightweight brown or black plant remains mixed through the soil. Such fine measurements are unnecessary for the gardener, but think of the particles as different-sized wet marbles in a jar. Clay particles, the smallest, fit close together, so it takes a large number to fill the jar. Since very small spaces are left between the particles, together they create a large surface area. Since water adheres to the soil particles, the amount of surface area will determine the quantity of water the soil can retain. The large "marbles" – grains of sand – leave large empty pockets because they do not pack in well together, so we have fewer marbles and less wet surface area but more space for air. The medium "marbles" – silt – fit somewhere in between.

Coarse-grained sandy soils, then, have lots of air space, which means that they dry quickly by allowing rain to drain freely. The fast drainage leaches out nutrients, however, making them poor soils that are low in nutrition, although they are easy to work. Clay soils, on the other hand, are cold, wet and hard to work; water clings to the surface of the fine-particled clay, excluding air and making it very difficult for rain to drain away. It has been estimated that water moves down through sand at the rate of 750 feet per day, but it penetrates only 6 inches through clay in the same time. When dry, however, clay soils resemble nothing so much as cracked concrete.

A simple test will give a reasonable indication of the makeup of your soil. Take a trowelful of soil from the area in question, and remove obvious "impurities" such as pebbles, beetles and worms. Allow the sample to dry until it can be rubbed into a fine powder. Then fill a straight-sided glass jar about two-thirds full of water, and add the soil sample. Screw the lid on tightly, and shake the jar vigorously. Let it stand undisturbed until the soil has settled and the water cleared. Sand will settle out immediately, but it may take two days for everything to settle and the

9

Whether you are choosing plants for sun or shade, soil composition must be con-sidered. Shade-loving rhododendrons and azaleas do especially well in acidic soils.

water to clear. A layer of humus will float on the top of the water, while on the bottom of the jar, there will be a layer of sand topped by silt and then clay particles.

A soil that shows 50 to 70 percent sand with a content of less than 15 percent clay and the rest silt is known as sandy soil. Large amounts of humus will be needed to improve its moisture- and nutrient-holding capacity. Where practical, adding some clay to this type of soil will also be of great benefit.

Sandy loam, with 35 to 50 percent sand and more clay and silt, is a good soil, especially if the humus content is high. Silty loam, with about 50 percent silt and 15 to 25 percent clay, is also a good rich soil, but it tends to go lumpy when dry. Adding river-washed sand to improve the drainage will make it a very good soil.

A clay soil, composed of mostly clay and silt, is the most difficult type to cope with, but if properly worked, it can be incredibly rich and productive. Basic clay soil is cold and wet in the spring and often water-logged, yet it bakes into a hard, solid mass in the summer. A word to the wise: Never work a clay soil when it is wet, because that simply compounds the problem. Leaving it rough-dug to weather in the fall will improve the structure in the short term. Applying lime in early spring will have the same effect, causing the clay particles to flocculate, or combine to form sand-sized lumps. One treatment will last for several years. Working in large quantities of humus and river-washed sand or even gravel, if it is not too coarse (a quarter-inch pebble is the largest useful size), will greatly improve drainage and air penetration and will also help to free up nutrients locked in the clay.

Old-timers talked of soils in terms of their being "sour" or "sweet" and would test theirs by tasting it. But testing has since grown far more sophisticated, and new gardeners are often mystified by references to a soil's "pH." The measurement of relative acidity or alkalinity is expressed in terms of its pH, the scale of which ranges from 1 to 14, with pH 7 being neutral and pH 8 alkaline. The preferred range for most plants is between 5.5 and 7.5, but there are some exceptions. Azaleas, blueberries and rhododendrons, for example, demand acidic conditions and will thrive with a soil pH as low as 4.5. Soil pH is not, in my opinion, something to lose sleep over, and I recommend ignoring it as long as things are going well. When plants do not thrive, though, check the soil pH as a possible cause. If the soil is found to be very acidic or very alkaline, it will affect the type of plants that can be grown, but choosing plants to suit the soil is far easier than making any major changes in the soil's pH. Advanced gardeners growing specialized collections of plants will perhaps have to pay special attention to soil pH, but for our purposes, simple soil-testing kits can be obtained from most garden stores.

Lawns

The shade gardener enjoys choice about many things, but there is one hard fact that must be accepted from the outset: a first-class lawn, one that will stand up to heavy wear and tear, is impossible in a shaded area. The deeper the shade, the

In untravelled areas, flowering ground covers are a pleasing alternative to grass.

more difficult it is to grow decent grass, and no good turf grass will tolerate dense shade. A lawn is a collection of individual, tough, resilient, sun-loving grass plants. When denied good light conditions, they tend to grow tall, spindly and weak, just as tomatoes or any other sun worshippers do. The result is reduced tolerance to heat, cold, drought, disease and foot traffic. Although this paints a bleak picture, there are steps that can be taken to reduce the stress and make a presentable lawn possible. (Just as important, however, are the strategies you can use in high-traffic areas. Be sure to plan for tougher lawn substitutes, such as pavers, gravel or bark chips. Consider massed ground covers such as lily-of-the-valley or crown vetch in areas traditionally designated as lawn but not used by the family, such as the front garden.)

The first and most essential step is to use top-quality, shade-tolerant grass varieties and to choose a blend suitable for the situation. No single grass type can cope with all the variations of climate and usage to which lawns are exposed, so lawn seed is blended by the seed companies to fit different situations. For a lawn that will be partly in shade and partly in sun, use a seed mix containing types suitable for both. As the lawn becomes established, the shade-tolerant grasses will thrive in

11

An arbour affords home gardeners a chance to devise their own shady areas.

contents. The pedigree grasses will have the variety name along with the type of grass. For example, one of the new-generation grasses is 'Vista' creeping red fescue; the older type will simply be listed as creeping red fescue. The percentage of each grass in the mix will also be on the label. While there is nothing wrong with the nonpedigree mixes, when it comes to growing in less than good conditions, the pedigree grasses have a definite edge. Beware of bargain-basement-priced seed, because the quality of grass seed varies and a mix can contain weed grasses such as crab grass. As the saying goes, you get what you pay for.

Shady conditions are often associated with restricted air movement, which results in an increase in the relative humidity, the slow drying of dew or other moisture on the turf and a prolonged period of conditions that favour disease development. Anything that increases air circulation, such as the removal of low-hanging tree branches or the thinning out of shrubs and underbrush, will help the lawn. Small adjustments in what we regard as normal lawn culture will pay big dividends:

1. Avoid watering unless the turf is obviously suffering from drought, and then apply at least an inch of water. Try to irrigate during midmorning to reduce the length of time the grass is wet.

2. Fertilizer should be reduced to approximately half of that used on a full-sun area. Apply the fertilizer in early spring before the trees leaf out and again in autumn when the leaves are falling.

3. The recommended mowing height is at least 3 inches, an inch or so above the normal mowing height for turf in full sun. Never cut shaded turf when it is wet.

4. Route foot traffic away from areas of shaded turf.

5. Remove leaves, debris and litter on a regular basis to prevent smothering of the grass and interruption in the availability of light.

6. Establishing or repairing a lawn by seeding or sodding is best done in late summer. This allows the longest period of

the shaded areas while the sun-loving grasses will take over in the sunny spots.

The one spot in which I would forgo using a blend is in medium-to-heavy dry shade, such as under a maple tree. Here I would use Chewings fescue, an extremely shade-tolerant grass with good disease resistance and drought tolerance that performs best on 50 percent of the normal application of lawn fertilizer. A very fine-textured grass that does not take hard wear, it is a lawn for looking at rather than using.

Extensive research in recent years has produced a new generation of grasses that are more tolerant of stress and have better resistance to the pests and diseases that can plague lawns. Read the package when shopping for lawn seed, and look for these new pedigree seeds. It is not necessary to know all the variety names, which in any case will differ according to area and seed company. Look for a package labelled as shade lawn grass, or sun and shade, and then look for a listing of the

Island beds and borders are perfect solutions for the grass-weary gardener. This curving pathway leads us past gardens planted beneath maturing trees.

time for establishment and growth under good light conditions.

Garden Style

My gardens are never designed. Instead, they evolve as new ideas and interests come along and are integrated or rejected. They give great pleasure, and I am always happy with the outcome; yet I still wonder how things would turn out if I were disciplined enough to draw up a master plan and stick to it.

The principles of good design are applicable to any garden and can be found in numerous books. They are worth studying, especially when you are planning a new garden from scratch, but they often appear complex and daunting to a beginner. Learn from them, but keep in mind that the garden is yours to do with as you please. Thomas Church, one of the foremost American landscape designers of the 20th century, held that landscaping should be logical, down-to-earth and aimed at making your plot of ground produce exactly what you want and need from it. He said, "There are no mysterious 'musts,' no set rules, no finger of shame pointed at the gardener who doesn't follow an accepted pattern." Church knew a garden was a success only if it pleased the user, and he never lost sight of the fact that gardens, whether large or small, are for people.

When creating a garden, the best advice I can give is to take it slowly. Allow plenty of time to ask yourself questions, to gather your thoughts and to give ideas a chance to sink in. In order for the garden to succeed, both people and plants must be happy, so you should always keep in mind both what the garden will be used for and who will spend time there. Be realistic. A mustn't-touch garden can be tolerated for an hour's visit to Grandma, but don't expect children to live in one. Plants and kids can get along fine, provided we have the foresight to cater to play. Even the thoughtful design of a simple path can make a big difference. A circular route

13

Pastel-coloured furniture brightens this shady corner by reflecting the available light, while impatiens happily grow, tucked beneath shrubs and vines.

made for tearing around and around on tricycles will amuse small children for hours at a stretch, but a straight path ending at a garden seat can lead to boredom. Sandboxes can be designed and built with an eye to converting the site into a water feature later. Any plans for family dining al fresco, entertaining friends or providing a quiet corner to relax in should be considered from the outset, even if it will take time before they can be implemented. These strictures apply to any type of garden planning, in sun or shade.

When working with shade, however, the scale and proportions of the garden are usually predetermined by the very trees or walls that provide the shade. Our task is to recognize the potential of what is there and to decide how best to use it. An area completely surrounded by tall buildings may be in solid shade but will be open to the sky above, and a fair amount of light will penetrate to the ground. A favourite restaurant in Kingston, Ontario, has turned just such an unprepossessing site into one of the most inviting outdoor eating areas I know of. Narrow raised beds around the perimeter are planted with grapevines trained to form a canopy, while the central area has rows of small-leafed trees.

This simple treatment provides a light, airy effect of dappled green shade, at the same time effectively blocking out unattractive surroundings.

What an exciting challenge a shaded, hemmed-in yard in the city is. This is the one shade situation where gardeners have complete freedom to choose their gardens' style. Such a space can be strictly formal or casually informal, or it can be the controlled chaos of a rambling wilderness. It can become a sophisticated entertainment area in a shaded courtyard, paved with granite slabs, embellished with elegant wrought-iron furniture and dressed with ground covers such as 'Beacon Silver' dead nettle (*Lamium*) or sweet woodruff, formal-looking perennials like hostas or the rusty foxglove (*Digitalis ferruginea*) and carefully trained climbers. A small fountain cascading into a classic pool would add a feeling of cool serenity and help mask traffic noise. Concrete pavers, a built-in brick barbecue, a wooden picnic table and beds of cheery impatiens may better suit the budget and life style of a young family. Raised flowerbeds behind walls built wide enough to take cushions would provide plenty of extra seating for informal entertaining. Use tough plants such as bugleweed for areas of ground covers. They will stand the occasional forgetful child running across them.

Painting the walls white or a pastel shade will brighten the area by reflecting the light from above. Using pale-coloured paving stones or gravel, introducing mirrors or the newly popular old-fashioned mirror spheres into the design or adding a pool to reflect light are other ideas that will drastically decrease the density of the shade. Add a trellis with climbing plants, and some character begins to emerge. A wide selection of trellis patterns is available, both to buy and to make, but consider their differing effects before deciding on one. White diamond trellis over a yellow wall can bring the feeling of a sunny conservatory. Paint the same walls white, allow the unpainted trellis to turn to a natural weathered grey, choose shrubs and perennials with an emphasis on attracting birds and butterflies, and a wildlife garden begins to take shape. Good choices of plants would include dogwood, Oregon grape, February daphne, lily-of-the-valley and meadow-rue.

The options are not quite so numerous when the source of the shade is trees. Unless the trees were planted as part of a formal design, formality is difficult to achieve. Forget the regimental rows of tulips lined up in their scarlet uniforms – they are for the brazen sun. Think instead of pale, cool colours and a soft natural look to emphasize the woodsy nature of the shade and

The positioning of paths lends ambience to a garden setting; here, a visitor can wander through an arbour into the nether reaches of the garden.

to produce an atmosphere of serenity. The minimalist gardener can create a restful, low-maintenance sanctuary to retreat to at the end of a working day. Consider an area of ancient-looking cobblestones, easily achieved with modern cobblestone pavers, and surround it with carpets of sturdy ground covers like wild ginger (*Asarum*), double bloodroot or foamflower. You might also consider adding a garden seat to one side and an interesting focal point such as a handsome birdbath or sculpture. Your sanctuary will then become an oasis of green quietude.

A keen gardener will take the opposite tack. The shade garden offers scope to grow dozens of wonderful sun-shy plants. Primulas (which range all the way from the tiny *Primula rosea* to the majestic candelabras), foamflowers, barrenworts, *Iris cristata*, trilliums, hepaticas, anemonellas and many others will thrive here. With these gardeners, space will be grudgingly given to narrow paths – or perhaps only strategically placed steppingstones – to al-

low access to these gems of the shade, and the gardener will then spend every spare hour either working with or gloating over his or her treasures.

A collector naturally puts plants above everything, but in general, it is wise to remember that paths play an important role and can make or mar a garden. Main paths should be functional and must follow the pattern of traffic in the garden to be of use. We have all seen the picturesque path wending and winding its way to the door, invariably accompanied by the worn grooves in the lawn where the family cuts straight across from the gate. Paths should also be wide enough to allow comfortable passage, whether you are taking a stroll or pushing a laden wheelbarrow. With the day-to-day usage catered to, secondary paths can be added at will, but I always feel a path needs a purpose. It may draw the eye to a special focal point, meander alongside a stream or simply lead to a garden seat, but there should be a reason to walk down a path.

Stones act as a low-maintenance ground cover in a setting of mixed shade; this reflecting pool transforms a garden into a place for quiet contemplation.

To create a garden in an area of shade is to journey down an intriguing path, the pathway of discovery. When approached with an open mind, it is the most valuable path to tread in the making of any garden. Along the way, we learn that the stuff under our feet is not dirt but living soil which, if nurtured and cared for, will grow in strength and blossom forth like a well-loved child. We also begin to notice that shade is not gloomy, after all, but consists of interesting variations and depths of light. As we delve into books and catalogues or visit gardens, we gradually discover a wealth of plants that even welcome our shade. Finally, the penny drops, and we realize how fortunate we are to have a shady spot in which to garden.

Lancelot "Capability" Brown, the great 18th-century landscaper, had the right idea. When faced with a new site, no matter how daunting, he would gaze around and declare, "The place has capabilities." I would like to see his signature phrase become a rallying call to replace the gloom-and-doom attitude to gardening in the shade. As we are beginning to see, the shaded area does indeed have capabilities, and it is the gardener who must uncover them.

Chapter One:
City Shade
By David Tomlinson

Gardening in a hot, harsh urban environment is without a doubt a daunting challenge. At the same time, it offers an alluring promise: the prospect of turning a patch of concrete jungle into an enticing paradise for family and friends. ✍ Shade is always welcome in the torrid summer heat of the city, but the thought of trying to garden in the shade dismays many people. City shade has a different dimension than that of the woodland. In the downtown core, while trees may be a factor, much of the shade actually comes from tall buildings, walls and fences. They cast a solid shade, and often, no direct sunlight reaches the garden. But because the area is open to the sky, it will usually receive quite bright light from above. ✍ For the city gardener, soil can be more of a problem than shade. Deprived of the natural accumulation of humus from plant and animal remains and sheltered from rain by roofs, walls and hard surfaces, much of the soil has become dry and impoverished. Walls absorb moisture from the soil, creating particularly poor growing conditions at their base. Yet when soil improvement and watering is undertaken, a border along the base of a wall can be one of the best growing areas in the garden. (In newer subdivisions, even more difficult conditions prevail. Contractors often use the garden to bury unwanted building materials, over which they spread what some-

A mock orange fronted by hostas and ferns is an unusual foundation planting.

best locations I have in the entire garden for growing ferns, primulas, Jack-in-the-pulpits and other shade-loving plants. East-facing walls produce semishaded conditions, and the heavily shaded area behind the north wall has the coolest growing conditions to be found in my garden. On the south and west sides, the house walls reflect sunlight, which in turn heats the ground below, providing ideal conditions for early spring-flowering bulbs that enjoy the warmth the walls generate.

The heat that escapes through the house foundations in winter can be another influencing factor, since it creates relatively frost-free conditions, particularly close to the walls. Plants that are not considered hardy in your climatic zone will very often grow successfully here. Abandon the dreary evergreens and be adventurous – look around the garden centre and browse through mail-order catalogues to find some of the more interesting plants that can be grown around the foundations of your house.

Walls and Fences

The walls of the house are yet another neglected microclimate. Ideal for vines, the shaded east side of our house is where we grow the climbing hydrangea, one of the best of the self-clinging, shade-loving vines, which produces its white flowers in July and August. Although it eventually climbed, it required a supporting trellis for several years before developing self-clinging rootlike holdfasts.

Trees are traditionally used to give shade, but it is possible to have shade without them. As we have found, all gardens have some shade provided by the walls of the house, and this shade can be utilized. More shade can be created by timber boundary fences, screen trellises, arbours or hedges. When garden buildings such as gazebos, toolsheds and pool changing rooms are needed, a thoughtful choice of site can greatly increase the amount of usable shade without your having to wait the years it can take for trees

times seems like a merely symbolic amount of topsoil.)

By deflecting winds, encouraging snow buildup and reflecting winter sunshine, walls and fences can produce microclimates where the growing environment is significantly different from that enjoyed by the general area. Often, this is enough to enable plants to survive outside their accepted hardiness zone and to give the novice gardener the thrill of being the first one on the block with crocuses in bloom. Whatever the current condition of your garden, take heart – nearly all the lovely gardens that now grace our cities began as miserable building sites.

Foundation Planting

Begin by assessing what you have. If your lot is in an established neighbourhood, it has probably already been landscaped with a mediocre lawn and the inevitable foundation plants. In my opinion, traditional foundation planting is a huge waste of the most sheltered growing area in a garden. Our small house has a five-foot-wide border along the walls, where we manage to grow more than 150 different kinds of plants, including rare and unusual shade lovers, in place of the usual dusty and predictable evergreens.

The north and east sides are by far the

The walls of a house are ideal for shade-loving vines such as the climbing hydran-gea, which, after a little support early on, will develop its own adhesive system.

and shrubs to develop. For example, a solid timber fence erected along the southern boundary will provide a narrow border of dense shade within your garden, while a fence placed along the northern boundary has just the opposite effect – it provides a very hot, sunny border facing the garden. Along the eastern boundary, a fence creates a border that is shady in the morning and sunny in the afternoon, while a fence on the west side does the reverse.

Not surprisingly, the height of the fence will also greatly influence the area of shaded ground – the higher the fence, the wider the shaded area. Even when you are desperate to produce some shade in your new garden, though, you must remember that many towns have height restrictions on fences. Check the bylaws of your local municipality before you build.

Another important consideration is that solid fences create very dense shade, and many plants prefer dappled shade. You can get the best of both worlds by designing a fence with the lower two-thirds constructed of solid board and the upper section of open trelliswork. This gives an area of dense shade close to the fence and an area of dappled shade in front, while allowing some air to pass freely through the fence. (Good air circulation is important in combating mildew and other fungal diseases.) I prefer this proportion to a half-and-half construction, because, to my eye, it is more aesthetically pleasing.

While the chain-link fences that divide the gardens in many new subdivisions create very little shade, you can easily convert them to denser shade-producing barriers by growing annual and perennial vines over them. Annual climbers such as canary creeper and scarlet runner bean will clothe the fence for the first year or two while more permanent plants become established. A very quick and permanent living fence can be obtained by planting silver lace vine (*Polygonum aubertii*), a vine which grows so rapidly that it often achieves 10 feet of growth in a season; it produces lacy white flowers in September. Most other perennial vines, such as Virginia creeper and clematis, are suitable, but they take a little longer to cover a chain-link fence.

Choosing the Right Spot

When selecting locations for some of the harder-to-grow plants like primulas, which require very specific growing conditions, it is important to find spots that remain cool during hot summer weather. Predictably, the coolest spots are normally found in the shadiest areas, although wind movement and the moisture content of the soil will also have an effect. When using reference books to check specific growing requirements, bear in mind that many books on gardening have been written for British gardeners, and the light and climatic conditions in Britain are vastly different from those found in North America. Excellent information can be gleaned from these books, provided one can translate it, so to speak, into local conditions.

Our garden, Merlin's Hollow, is located in Aurora, in southern Ontario, which is at the same latitude as Milan in northern Italy. Most of eastern Canada is well south of Britain, whereas Winnipeg, Regina, Calgary and much of southern British Columbia are almost at the same latitude as the south coast of Britain. This means that the sunlight in the southern parts of eastern Canada is much more powerful than in Britain, and plants recommended for sunny locations in Britain often need to be planted in semishade or shifting shade. This also applies to planting in the prairies, for there is little or no cloud in these areas, while Britain is often very overcast. The only area with a climate similar to that of Britain is the coastal area of British Columbia, where many of the most impressive gardens in Canada are to be found.

Shade Trees

When considering new trees to provide future shady areas, put a good deal of thought into their selection and placement within the garden, considering both practical and aesthetic aspects. You may be fond of maples, but they give a dense, dry shade that makes the cultivation of lawns and perennials beneath them extremely difficult. Likewise, crab apple trees, while beautiful in flower, have fruit that drops in the fall and may encourage mice to take up residence.

Few trees are necessary to shade an average-sized subdivision garden, but young nursery trees look small and insignificant, so there is a great temptation to plant several to create the sense that the lot is well treed. Unfortunately, little trees eventually grow into large ones that are difficult and expensive to remove. The first rule, therefore, is to plant carefully with a long-term view in mind. In the early years, you will have lots of sunny areas, but gradually, as the trees mature, the amount of shade they cast will increase. As the light and shade conditions change, it will be necessary to adjust the planting in your garden. In the long run, then, it is far better to plant one potentially large tree (or two or three medium-sized trees) and then wait patiently for them to grow than to fill the garden with trees to get a quick effect.

In late spring, the laburnum's yellow flowers and leaves cast a dense shade for part of the day that even sun lovers such as tulips and alliums can appreciate.

If you are choosing one large tree, my personal recommendation would be an oak. Most of the oak species are suitable: they have high-branching crowns, cast a light shade and have a deep root system. Their only drawback is that their leaves contain a large amount of tannin and therefore rot slowly. Oaks are also an excellent choice because of their attractiveness to wildlife – many species of birds, mammals and insects feed on their leaves and acorns. Ash trees and honey locusts also cast a light shade, but the honey locust has a shallow root system. In a small garden, birch trees are a fine choice, but unfortunately, these and the honey locust are subject to a stem borer that kills many trees just when they become large enough to cast the right degree of shade. Avoid the European birch (*Betula pendula*) and plant the beautiful native canoe bark birch (*B. papyrifera*), which is more resistant to the borer.

I have had a lot of success with the northern catalpa (*Catalpa speciosa*). A very fast-growing shade tree with large leaves and lovely flowers in early July, the catalpa's rapid growth quickly brings shade to a treeless site. My tree is now 12 years old and is 25 to 30 feet high. The first branch is over 15 feet above the ground, which allows light and moisture to penetrate. Normally, this tree would be lower branched, but over the past eight years, I have carefully retained the main leader and removed one low branch each year; now, it has a good, clean, tall trunk. As well, it has the advantage of leafing out very late, thus allowing spring-flowering bulbs to develop and ripen their foliage before heavy shade is created.

Generally, I avoid conifers, although a well-spaced single row along the boundary of a large property works quite well. Odd ones planted among groups of deciduous trees can improve shade conditions, but pure stands of conifers, either pines or spruce, cast heavy year-round shade that few plants will tolerate.

When siting trees to provide shade, the

23

The shifting shade of the horse chestnut and the deep, predictable shade of the hemlock and spruce, more often found in woodlands, lend serenity to this city lot.

ideal situation to aim for is one of shifting shade. This means that for some part of the day, most plants are in the shade of a wall, trellis, fence or tree, while at other times, they are in full sun.

If you are not sure how a particular tree location affects the movement of shade within your garden, make a simple ⅛-to-12-inch scale model of it. To represent the trees, use dry flower heads of yarrow, goldenrod or Queen Anne's lace. Scale the flower heads to the height of the tree at maturity – a birch would grow to about 25 feet high, so a 3-inch-tall flower stem and head would be to the correct scale. Glue

the flower stem upright in your selected tree location. Move a high-intensity light over the model, following the sun's daily path. Start with the light low in the east, then move it high in the south and low again in the west, and see where the shadows are cast at different times of the day.

By varying the height of the light, you can also study the different shade patterns in winter and summer. Since the sun is lower in the sky in winter, the shaded areas are increased. This can be an important factor in your being able to maintain snow cover over tender plants, since the extra shade prevents the accumulated

24

snow from melting too quickly during midwinter or early-spring thaws.

Shrubs for Shade

In a small city garden, plant tall-growing shrubs instead of trees. These will cast enough shade to allow you to grow a wide variety of plants under and between them. Selecting shrubs with this purpose in mind is not difficult in eastern Canada, the northeastern United States or the West Coast but can present difficulties in the prairie regions, where fewer shrubs survive the extreme winter conditions.

In the Northeast, there are several reliable shrubs that tolerate a wide range of soil and moisture conditions and can be used either to provide patches of shade or to grow in the shade of existing trees. The native highbush cranberry (*Viburnum trilobum*) and the wayfaring tree (*V. lantana*) are particularly useful. I also like the lesser-known serviceberry (*Amelanchier alnifolia*), with its early white flowers. The variegated types of dogwood are a good choice as well – they keep their coloured leaves in shade rather than reverting to all green; some varieties have colourful winter twigs; and all have berries that are attractive to birds.

An interesting fall-flowering shrub is the witch hazel (*Hamamelis virginiana*). An asset to most gardens, it has foliage like that of a common hazel but also has good fall colour and fragrant, yellow, ribbonlike flowers in October after leaf fall. The more tender Chinese witch hazel (*H. mollis*), with larger, showier flowers, grows on the West Coast.

Prairie gardeners, as I have mentioned, have a more difficult task, as their list of suitable shade trees and tall shrubs is not very extensive. Aspens (*Populus tremuloides*), crab apples and mountain ash are extremely hardy and cast a light shade. Lilacs and the ubiquitous pea shrub (*Caragana arborescens*) are indestructible even in the most inhospitable new subdivision. Try the more elegant open-spreading Lorberg's pea shrub (*C. a. lorbergii*), which is less

This yard features the vibrant blossoms of azalea, rhododendron and dogwood.

dense and coarse than the common pea shrub and creates a lighter, dappled shade. The serviceberry also does well in western gardens, where the native silver-leafed buffalo berry (*Shepherdia argentea*) can be used to good effect. Except for the lilac, the pea shrub and the buffalo berry, most of these shrubs are reasonably shade-tolerant and will increase the density of the shade under tall, high-branched trees.

Improving Existing Shade

If you already have a lot with well-established shade trees, you can provide nearly ideal growing conditions for many shade-loving plants. First, take a long, hard look at your trees. If thinning is necessary, either seek the help of a professional or deal with it yourself. Study the trees carefully, however, before you start to prune. The aim is to remove only the minimum number of branches to provide pools of dappled shade beneath them.

Improving the quality of the soil under 25

Choose plants like these Japanese maples that will both benefit from existing shade and create new shade in which lower-growing plants will flourish.

your trees is vital to the health of your shade garden. Urban gardeners tend to be a particularly tidy-minded lot, conscientiously raking up every fallen leaf and twig they can find, only to abandon these riches by the curb for the garbage pickup. This practice, dutifully carried out over the years, gradually robs the soil under the trees of all fertility. It must be remembered that the roots of trees are constantly removing moisture, minerals and plant food from the soil. In the wild, when leaves fall, they lie and rot. Minerals are thereby returned to the ground, and a moisture-holding organic layer of soil slowly builds up under the tree. It is this layer that eventually supports the shade-loving plants. If you continually remove the fallen leaves, nothing is being returned to the soil. This is a problem that can't be overemphasized to the shade gardener, and there is a simple solution: do the opposite of your neighbours. When they put out their leaves for the garbage, collect and compost them to build up the soil layer in your garden. Leaf mould, gardener's gold, is yours for the making.

Making Leaf Mould

Build two 4-by-4-foot bays using iron T-bars or pressure-treated 2-by-4-inch posts and galvanized wire fencing. Place the leaves in compacted layers about 12 inches deep, making sure they are wet (this is very important for speedy decomposition). Scatter a 4-inch-diameter plant pot full of nitrate of ammonia over each layer, repeating the operation until the bay is full.

It takes about 12 months for the leaves to turn into usable leaf mould; consider it ready when it looks like dark chocolate cheesecake. Two bays are required so that you can be filling one while using the leaf mould in the other. Leaf mould is by far the best soil conditioner to use under trees. When it is ready, spread the heap under your trees. Repeat this annually, distributing the compost carefully between, not over, established plants, and let the tree's natural leaf fall remain on the ground under the tree.

Making leaf mould takes time; until it is available, the next best material to use is composted cow or sheep manure, which can be purchased in bags from garden centres. Peat moss is frequently recommended as a good stand-in for leaf mould. While it is easy to handle and readily available, peat moss is not really an adequate substitute, though, unless you are growing rhododendrons or other acid-loving plants. Its main disadvantage is that once it dries out, it is difficult to get it moist again. If you have to use peat moss, keep the ground under the trees well watered. All perennials grown under trees need regular watering, particularly in spring and early summer, when they are growing rapidly and producing flowers. You can reduce watering as the summer progresses, unless you are growing some of the more delicate plants such as primulas, which need a lot of moisture.

Choosing the Right Plant

After the hard work comes the reward: choosing plants for your shade beds. Annuals can provide interest and colour until the perennial plants are established and can also be used to good effect in late summer and early fall when few perennial shade plants are in flower. I'm especially fond of tobacco plants, and there are some good dwarf forms, known as 'Nicki' and 'Domino' hybrids, in shades of pink, red, lime and white. If I could grow only one, however, it would be the splendid late-flowering Indian tobacco (*Nicotiana sylvestris*). This stately 5-foot-tall sculptural plant has large, light green leaves and clusters of extremely fragrant, long, white, tubular flowers. I grow it by the side door, where its wonderful scent greets me whenever I enter or leave the house in the evening.

Forget-me-nots, although attractive, are a two-edged sword. Gardeners either love them or hate them. They colonize damp shade well, but if left to their own devices, they will romp all over the garden. Look for the pink and white varieties. To retain these, it is essential to remove all blue-flowering seedlings systematically, or your planting will gradually revert back. As an alternative, try *Brunnera macrophylla*, which can best be described as a clump-forming perennial forget-me-not. Another easy plant similar to forget-me-not is the low-growing blue-eyed Mary (*Omphalodes verna*), which does well in dry shade and spreads slowly.

An overhead tree casts shade on fox-gloves, hostas, irises and bellflowers.

Petunia hybrids also do remarkably well in light shade, as do annual phlox and garden verbena. Bedding pansies and violas can be used to provide patches of early and late colour, since many of the newer varieties will bloom in the spring and again in the fall.

Over the years, I've had difficulties overwintering biennial foxgloves in my fertile soil. Well-grown plants with lush, leafy rosettes inevitably suffer winterkill. This will also be the fate of *Digitalis mertonensis*, a beautiful foxglove with crushed-strawberry-coloured flowers. I have found the best way to grow these is to keep them in a 4-inch pot until late summer and then plant them in their flowering position. This allows them to root well before winter but does not give them sufficient time 27 to put on excessive soft, leafy growth, something that may not be a problem in poor, sandy soils. The yellow foxglove (*D. grandiflora*) is a different story altogether. An exceedingly hardy, good-natured perennial, it never fails to produce a mass of soft creamy-yellow flowers in July and August. No self-respecting shade bed should be without a good-sized clump.

Probably the two most extensively planted groups of perennials are the reliable and easily cultivated day lilies, which are now available in many colours and heights, and the hostas, which have an almost infinite variety of leaf patterns. Both tolerate a wide range of soil and shade conditions, including comparatively dry shade.

Primulas are a rather exacting but rewarding group of plants with which to experiment. Providing you grow them in a rich, organic, leafy soil and prevent them from drying out, they will normally thrive in dappled shade. Other plants that grow particularly well with primulas are Jack-in-the-pulpits. The native North American *Arisaema triphyllum* will grow in ordinary soil in perennial borders, where the shade of surrounding perennial plants seems to suit it admirably.

Several years ago, I imported from Britain a tuber of the most beautiful *Arisaema* of them all, *A. sikokianum*. This plant has a startlingly contrasting flower of purple-brown and pure white. I carefully planted my expensive tuber. It was in the ground for a mere 12 hours when a squirrel dug it up and ate it – a costly lunch for me to provide. Squirrels display a noticeable preference for the bulbs and corms of European and Asian plants; only occasionally do they choose to eat the native plants. A biologist friend speculates that over the course of their evolution, our native plants may have developed toxins which the squirrels find repulsive. If these toxins could somehow be isolated, they could be used as an organic control to prevent the substantial damage done by squirrels in urban gardens.

Another good group of flowering plants is the woodland geraniums. The pale mauve native geranium (*Geranium maculatum*) flowers well but does best in locations that get at least three hours of direct sunlight a day. In areas of deeper shade, *G. macrorrhizum*, which is found wild in the Balkan peninsula in Europe, is much more tolerant. It produces masses of pale pink flowers in late May and June, and its foliage, unlike that of our wild geranium, remains green throughout the summer. A very good cultivar of this plant is 'Ingwersen's Variety,' which has recently been introduced to the Canadian market.

Our native foamflower (*Tiarella cordifolia*) spreads slowly into a carpet of soft green leaves that is covered with a mass of white foamy flowers in May. A lesser-known relative, *T. wherryi*, forms neat clumps of typical foamflower leaves topped with spikes of pink-tinged flowers in spring. This plant was crossed with coral bells (*Heuchera sanguinea*) at a large British nursery, and the result of this cross, *Heucherella* 'Bridget Bloom,' is starting to appear in Canadian garden centres. It produces pink flowers over a long period, as do the many varieties of red, pink and white coral bells.

Another spreading plant that, if left to its own devices, will form an attractive ground cover, is the very fragrant sweet woodruff (*Galium odoratum*). While it has a reputation for being extremely invasive, it can be kept under control quite easily if excessive growth is forked out once a year in midsummer. The wonderful fragrance of its small clusters of white flowers makes it worth the extra attention, and it will grow in the deepest shade. Avoid the common lily-of-the-valley unless you have a place in a wild garden where it can spread without creating a problem.

Most of the shade-loving perennials flower in early spring and summer, and it is often difficult to find ones that bloom in mid-to-late summer and fall. One of the best plants to fill this bill is the Turk's cap lily (*Lilium martagon*), which is found throughout Europe and northern Asia. The true species has a dull red, black-spotted nodding flower with reflexed pet-

A tree eventually matures and creates shade. A fence, however, instantly provides a setting for shade-loving plants that doesn't compete for soil moisture.

als. It has been extensively hybridized and is now available in a wide range of red, pink and white flowers. The white form (*L. m. album*) is particularly attractive. All these lilies, which can grow as tall as 3 to 4 feet, do well in deep shade.

Public interest in the shade-loving ferns reached its height in Victorian England, when ferneries were often a major feature of many quite small town gardens. In the long period between and just after the two World Wars, however, ferns went completely out of gardening fashion, although it is interesting to note that they are coming back into vogue. It was during this period that I unwittingly committed my greatest act of horticultural vandalism. The park where I worked held a considerable collection of rare ferns. They were grown in neat, labelled rows in deep shade behind the high brick wall of the old kitchen garden. Every few years, we would carefully dig them up and split, replant and label them. Although we did this job when directed by the district park

superintendent, who knew the value of this unique collection, we all felt it was a complete waste of time, as nobody was interested in ferns. Eventually, the old superintendent retired, and his successor ordered the ferns' removal. That day, I probably destroyed what was the most comprehensive collection of old fern varieties and cultivars in Britain. Through ignorance, I most likely brought about the extinction of some of the rarer forms. How I would like to have those old heritage plants in my shade bed today.

Fern cultivars are still difficult to obtain, but some garden centres do stock the delightful silver-and-green-leafed Japanese painted fern, which grows well in dryish shade. Several native ferns, such as the lovely maidenhair, are more readily available and well worth trying. Like the royal fern and the ostrich fern, the maidenhair enjoys a moist location with rich organic soil. I have seen the ostrich fern and royal fern growing in quite sunny or semishaded moist sites in the wild, but

29

A pocket of shade is a perfect home for the beautiful foliage of a potted coleus.

the maidenhair fern is certainly a plant of deep, moist shade. The best fern for dry shade is probably the male fern, which has large feathery fronds that cover a 3-foot-diameter area in my garden. But I have seen much larger plants in the wild.

Before purchasing any native plants, question the staff to make sure that the plants have been propagated in a nursery and not dug from the wild. Better still, learn to grow your own plants from spores or seeds.

Growing From Seed

Several years ago, I decided to try growing plants that are not normally available from local garden centres. I found that commercial nurseries and seed suppliers, with a few exceptions, offer a very limited range of unusual plants. The best way to obtain interesting seed, I found, was to join several of the specialist-plant societies that operate seed exchanges. Seed has many advantages when you wish to ac-

quire new and unusual plants. It is relatively inexpensive, and you can produce several plants that you can try out in different parts of the garden. You don't need a greenhouse or indoor growing facilities, because the seed can be germinated and grown outdoors with little fuss. Under normal conditions, you will get above-average results if you carefully follow these instructions:

1. When the seed arrives, store it in your freezer in a sealed plastic bag until you are ready to sow it.

2. Sow the seed in late September/early October or at least before the end of February.

3. Using a 4-inch pot or similar container with drainage holes, fill to within half an inch of the top with a moist soilless mix, firming it lightly.

4. Sow seed on the surface, and cover to about twice its diameter with mix shaken on top through a sieve. Very fine seed can be left uncovered.

5. Water the seed well, using a hand mister or a watering can with a fine spray head. Allow a couple of days for the seed to absorb moisture, and then place outside behind a north (preferable) or east wall or in some other very shaded location. Keep the seeded pots moist until mix freezes. Do not cover with polyethylene or other material, but allow the snow to drift in on top of them. If the seed is sown in winter, when the ground is covered with snow, put the pots in an unheated garage.

6. When the spring thaw arrives, check seed every day for germination. Move germinated seed to a sunnier location; shade plants can remain behind the north wall. Keep pots regularly watered before and after germination.

7. When the seedlings are large enough, with two or three leaves, they can be pricked out individually to 4-inch pots and allowed to continue growing until large enough to be planted in flowerbeds.

8. Guard against damage from slugs, earwigs and mice. I place treated bait in a pop can with an enlarged hole (to prevent birds from eating it) beside my seed pots—

Both impatiens and fuchsias can be either grown from seed or cuttings or purchased from nurseries. Each makes a colourful statement in a shady area.

seed you think hasn't germinated may already have been some predator's lunch!

9. In late May, move pots of ungerminated seed to a sunny location, and continue to keep moist.

Using this method, I have successfully germinated and established in my shade bed many species of otherwise unavailable plants. Germination times of seeds differ. Some discarded seeds have even germinated on our compost heap. If germination does not occur the first year, return pots to the shady area and keep for a second or even a third year.

The important thing about plants, planting and gardening in general is that you adopt an adventurous attitude. Don't believe anyone who says that shade limits the gardener. We have at present over 1,800 different perennial plants in our one-acre garden, and I still have several areas to develop. Only by buying unusual species will we encourage mail-order companies, nurseries and garden centres to carry a wider range of interesting plants. And only by constantly experimenting and extending the range and variety of plants that we grow will we allow our gardens to continue to evolve. So be adventurous, and have fun in the shade garden.

Chapter Two:
The Woodland Garden

By Bernard Jackson

ne of the very few good things I can say for World War II is that it was the cause of my being evacuated from a bomb-torn city into the peace and safety of the countryside. At the impressionable age of 6, I found myself in pastoral England, boarding in an old castle that was surrounded by green parkland, water, meadows and huge oaks, beeches and sycamores. I have loved such trees ever since. In fact, I cannot visualize, let alone feel comfortable in, a landscape without trees. ᐧᐧᐧ It is not surprising, then, that I think of trees as the backbone of the garden, the feature that above all else creates a sense of maturity and that ties the surrounding earth to the vast panorama of sky. Even on a new city building lot, stripped bare of everything green and pleasant, the planting of just a single small tree will alter one's whole impression of the site and establish a totally different ambience. ᐧᐧᐧ Some gardeners, nevertheless, continue to consider trees on their land a nuisance, in large part because of the shade these trees cast. While too many trees grown too closely together can indeed be a problem, it is a problem that is easily overcome – and overcome in such a way that the landowner can still gain benefit from retaining a carefully chosen percentage of them. Try to think of garden trees as old friends, and work with them rather than against them. Instead of curtailing gardening, trees provide the basis for a whole new sphere of gardening enjoyment. They are your chance to turn a mediocre landscape into a patch of beauty, mystery and delight.

There is also a practical value to be gained from the trees on your property. With the ever-rising cost of home heating, it may be well to remember that trees, correctly placed, will both cushion the house from cold winds in winter and shade it from excessive heat in summer. Trees also deaden the incoming noise that pollutes so much of our modern life, and as everybody knows, they help clean the very air we breathe.

For those gardeners like me who believe that a garden without wildlife is little more than a biological barren, trees have yet another advantage: they encourage a variety of creatures to make their home with us. There is no garden on Earth that cannot be improved by the singing of birds or the colour of butterflies among its flowers. And what is more pleasurable on a hot summer's day than to sit in the shade of a favourite tree, gently sipping a cup of tea or, perhaps, a glass of fine old whisky?

Types of Shade

Given the diversity of both sites and tree species, it should not come as too much of a surprise that there are likewise a number of different types of shade. Indeed, put a group of shade gardeners together, and one could easily start a lively discussion on the topic. For our purposes here, however, I shall discuss only three different, easily recognized types of tree shade: full shade, partial shade and dappled shade.

Full shade can be of two basic sorts. It can refer to the type of permanent shade that is to be found under a group of coniferous trees. Alternatively, it can mean the summer shade created by a very dense-leafed deciduous tree such as a beech. There are very few green plants that can survive in continuous deep shade. Some, such as trailing arbutus (*Epigaea repens*) and wood anemone (*Anemone nemorosa*), may try to creep in from the lighter pe-

riphery, but they will not enter far. Even the native mosses will slowly die out. In areas of extreme, constant shade, virtually nothing will grow.

With heavy summer shade, the situation is different: it is only at this time of year that there is not sufficient sunlight to sustain a ground cover. Plants such as the English and Spanish bluebells, Neapolitan cyclamen and shooting stars (*Dodecatheon* spp), which bloom in the spring or fall but rest in the summer, are quite at home with no summer sunshine. If your garden has a difficult spot created by a densely leafed deciduous tree, it would be wise to concentrate on spring- or fall-flowering plants that die down and rest after blooming.

Partial shade is found in areas where the sun reaches the ground for only part of the day, such as a site with an east or a west aspect. The term can also refer to a site that receives sunlight only during one season of the year, as with our site under the beech tree. Many plants grow very well when exposed solely to morning sunlight; indeed, the strong midday sun is detrimental to shade-loving plants.

A number of beautiful plants do well when restricted to morning sunlight. Among many others, some of the nicest include bleeding heart, astilbe, Christmas rose, gas plant, columbine, globeflower, summer phlox and giant rockfoil. Partial shade is, I think, the easiest type of shade for a gardener to handle.

Dappled shade refers to the mixture of light and shade caused by shafts of sunlight piercing the tree canopy or shooting through gaps between the trees. This is the type of shade I enjoy working with the most. I find such shade exciting, aesthetically pleasing and, to some extent, even ethereal; it creates an atmosphere in which one may just wonder whether there really are fairies at the bottom of the garden.

To add to its appeal, there are a lot of plants that respond to dappled shade: the lovely primroses and hostas in endless variety, violets, bloodroot, trilliums, Greek anemone, snowdrops, dogtooth violets, the gorgeous Himalayan poppy and the

There is an abundance of plants that will thrive in partial shade. Shown here are a vigorous pale pink astilbe, a delicate white columbine and a mountain bluet.

strangely appealing Jack-in-the-pulpit. These, and many more, can fill the shade gardener's hours with fun and fascination. Never turn your back on dappled shade, or you will be closing the door on a truly wonderful world.

Some Shade Problems

Our main concern when considering plants for shade must be whether they will get sufficient shade to meet their requirements or, conversely, whether there is still sufficient light available to allow them to function properly.

If your garden is too heavily shaded to grow much of anything well, then the shade will have to be reduced, either by actually thinning out the trees and shrubs or by pruning them to allow more light through the canopy. Seek some reliable advice on this matter; tree felling and high pruning require special skills, training and insurance, and it is usually wise to employ a professional for this work, especially if the work has to be done on an urban site where other houses or electrical wires could be damaged. If, on the other hand, the problem is simply a matter of dealing with a large shrub or small tree, it is easy

Both violas and periwinkle love the deep, damp organic soil of woodland areas.

of water making its way through, the competition for it will be great. Naturally enough, the trees themselves have prepared for this problem. As they have increased in size, they have also expanded their root systems to take advantage of available moisture and nutrients. While the roots of your plants will usually be close to the surface of the soil – and so closer to the incoming rain – the competition from tree roots is still a concern.

Most shade plants prefer a moist soil and a relatively high atmospheric humidity. For the practical gardener, this means that the soil must be checked regularly and given a deep soaking when necessary. It is far better to give the garden one really good soaking a week than to sprinkle it lightly every day. A regular light sprinkling will help maintain atmospheric humidity and benefit your shallow-rooted plants, but because of rapid summer evaporation, it will not do much for the deep-rooted plants or for the trees themselves.

It is important to provide ample water for the trees too; otherwise, they will act defensively and start sending more roots out to grab what water they can. This, of course, applies to the availability of nutrients as well. In areas where the soil is thin and tree-root systems naturally shallow, the tendency of the trees to send up feeder roots into any specially prepared soil is one of the most bothersome aspects of gardening under trees.

Water dripping from the leaves overhead can cause another problem, particularly during heavy rain. In addition to encouraging disease, it can wash the soil away from delicate surface roots and smash the blossoms as well. There is not much one can do to protect the blossoms, but a good surface dressing (also known as mulch) of partly decomposed leaves can stop the soil splatter and protect fragile roots from exposure.

enough to make your own adjustments.

Start by removing any deadwood that is present and then any branches which are growing inward. This may be all that is necessary. If not, remove some of the twigs from the bushier branches. If that fails to increase the incoming light adequately, start on the branches themselves, but remove them with discretion, remembering not to jeopardize the natural shape or balance of the tree. Always use sharp tools for the work, and make clean cuts. Although there is a difference of opinion among some experts, I prefer to treat any cut over an inch across with a good-quality tree paint. The debate over whether such action is necessary rages on, but at the very least, I feel that it makes the fresh cuts visually less obtrusive.

If you have ever sought shelter from a summer shower under a tree, you will have noticed just how little of the water actually reaches the ground. This is an important factor for the shade gardener to keep in mind. With such a small amount

What Type of Soil?

North America is a vast continent with a multitude of different geological regions

An adaptive gardener has made use of the moist, fertile pockets between these rocks to situate both purple and yellow groupings of primroses.

and habitats, which has resulted in a variety of soils. My soil, such as it is, is clayey and so has to be treated very differently from, say, a sandy soil.

It has been said that 95 percent of all tree roots are located within the top 4 feet of soil. If your garden possesses even half such a depth, then count your lucky stars and simply concentrate on improving the existing soil by adding liberal quantities of organic matter. However, if there is difficulty locating even 4 inches of topsoil, then most of your energy should be directed toward building up a greater soil depth so that you can grow anything at all. Unfortunately, shallow soils with trees growing on them are usually solid with an undesirable mass of fibrous roots. Often, the only way to overcome this problem is to build the soil up higher and then to feed and water it well to try to stop the tree roots from working up into this newly made environment.

Generally speaking, shade-loving plants respond best to soil that is rich in organic matter, whether it be leaf mould, peat, compost, old farmyard manure or a combination of any of these. Such soils are light, friable and capable of holding the necessary moisture and nutrients. Most soils respond favourably to the addition of organic matter; indeed, if your soil is sandy, liberal amounts of this material are essential. Woodland and other shade-loving plants usually keep their root systems within the top few inches of soil, so our efforts should be spent in looking after these few surface inches. Provided the lower depths are well drained, we need not worry too much about what is going on at the 2-foot level.

If the soil level beneath your trees has to be raised, it should be done only with light, porous mixes and then only to a depth of a few inches. If you add too much soil or soil that is too heavy to the ground beneath trees, there is a risk of stopping the necessary exchange of air to the established root system and possibly, in time, killing the tree. It is also important not to

37

The stone wall bordering this mulched path takes advantage of the garden's uneven terrain and gives the gardener a chance to show off annual colour.

allow the increased depth of soil to rest up around any tree trunks. Do not cover the area of trunk where it emerges from the soil. Instead, make a dry well of bricks, stones or hardwood boards at least a foot out from the trunk, and keep it well clear of weeds, fallen leaves or other garbage. If it is impractical to build a well around the trunk, then carefully slope the additional new soil away from it and upward onto the new bed.

Gardening in the shade is far more interesting if it encompasses the greatest possible variety of annual and perennial plants. Nonetheless, in this age of land shortages, population mobility, long-distance commuting and additional demands on leisure time, it would appear that what many people want is a quick, reliable and lasting splash of colour with the least possible amount of work. And who can blame them? There is no point putting a lot of effort into a more permanent planting if the family is likely to be transferred somewhere else or if it makes your only bit of leisure time a chore.

The answer to such a dilemma may be to plant annuals. The great advantage of annuals is that they stay in the soil for only one season, while perennials are there in-

Humans can short-circuit the natural energy cycle. When plants have been deprived of decomposing matter, soil should be supplemented with nutrients.

definitely. Thus the soil in an annual flowerbed can be dug over and any deficiencies rectified each year. If, for instance, you find that the drainage is poor or the soil would benefit from additional organic matter, it is relatively easy to fix these problems before the new crop of annuals goes in. Fortunately, many annuals have a profusion of beautiful blooms and a prolonged flowering period, especially if old flower heads are nipped off as they fade. Such plants as pansy, monkey flower, flowering tobacco and busy Lizzie (impatiens) are some annuals that come readily to mind for the shade garden.

Feeding Your Plants

Nothing will grow to its full potential without sufficient food, and that includes plants grown under trees. This comment may seem unnecessary, but the truth of the matter is that many people assume that because woodland plants in their natural setting thrive with no apparent as-sistance, garden plants grown in shade should do likewise. In the words of Cole Porter, "It ain't necessarily so." Wild plants are fed by nature. In addition to the steady, though admittedly small, amounts of animal manure, dead insects and so forth that perpetually supply the natural energy cycle, there is the annual leaf fall, which slowly but steadily breaks down and continuously releases its goodness back into the earth. With their roots close to the surface, woodland plants are the first to take advantage of this food supply.

Such a state of affairs could exist equally well under the trees in our gardens, but rightly or wrongly, we humans manage to get in the way. Not only do we have a tendency to crowd in more plants than would normally occur in nature, but most of us have a fetish for tidying up any leaf or small twig as soon as it hits the ground. Such compulsive behaviour disrupts the natural cycle and fouls up the ground's ability to look after its own. Thus it becomes necessary to feed our plants if they are to grow and flower according to our expectations.

If at all possible, this feeding should be done with organic manures rather than with commercial chemical fertilizers. This suggestion is not meant as a condemnation of chemical plant foods but simply as an acknowledgement that for this particular job, natural fertilizers are more effective because they improve the soil structure. I like to use a mixture of equal parts well-decomposed leaf mould and commercial composted sheep or cow manure. If leaf mould is in short supply, you could substitute ordinary garden compost. Spread the mixture an inch or two thick around each plant and over the soil surface in any gaps between plants. Do not cover the crowns of the plants, but tuck the material in gently beneath the leaves and among the stems around the crown.

Some people like to add a small amount of bone meal or even commercial fertilizer to this basic mixture, but be careful not to overdo it. Believe it or not, some plants can be killed with kindness. If you happen to be one of those lucky gardeners who can get their hands on quantities of old, well-seasoned farmyard manure, then use it. Remember, however, that horse manure is often full of grass seeds. Good old-fashioned cow manure with plenty of rotted straw mixed in is the best. It is worth its weight in gold.

If your garden is going to be situated under trees, it would pay to maintain a regular pile of leaf mould. In the fall, bags of fallen leaves can often be begged from neighbours or, in municipalities that don't operate a leaf-recycling scheme, picked up ahead of the garbage truck before they disappear into a landfill or go up in smoke.

Weeding

A weed is simply a plant growing out of place; even the most beautiful flower is a weed if it is growing in the wrong place at the wrong time. Whenever you notice such a plant, yank it out immediately. A weed left until later is usually a weed forgotten – forgotten, that is, until it has settled in permanently or, even worse, has sent hundreds or thousands of seeds all over the bed and among the crowns of your choicest flowers. I am not one for using chemical weedkillers, believing much more in the hand and the hoe. Yet if your garden becomes invaded by some vegetative terror such as goutweed, best head for a container of Clear-it, and be sure to read the directions on how to use it without destroying everything else.

Annual weeds pulled up before they have gone to seed can be relegated to the compost pile; their decomposed residue can later be recycled in a topdressing.

Maintenance

As long as your bed is regularly tended, it will require very little maintenance, particularly once the space is well filled with plants. Of course, there are some plants that need more attention than others; nonetheless, if one keeps ahead of the weeds, no big problem should arise. In my area, where there are regular intervals of prolonged heavy rain and where thick layers of wet, heavy snow often cover the ground for extended periods, soil compaction can be a problem. Apart from looking bad, compacted soil cannot breathe properly. Gently fluffing up the leafy soil with a cultivator or with your fingers usually remedies this problem. Nipping off all old flower heads as they fade will pay dividends in more flowers and stronger plants. If you want additional plants, it sometimes pays to leave the odd flower or two to go to seed and then let nature take its course through self-sowing.

Watch out for slugs, especially after a rain or when young shoots are pushing through the ground. These creatures, along with snails, can be especially bad during a mild, damp interval after a prolonged dry spell. If the use of poison bait is unacceptable, the next best thing is to destroy the slugs manually. Search for them in the evening or during damp weather, handpick them off the plant or ground, and then either squash them

Variegated leaves offer a cool respite in sunny areas; in darker spots, they intro-duce a welcome dimension of visual tex-ture when bright colour is not in evidence.

underfoot or drop them into a jar of salty water. Incidentally, salty water readily removes the slug slime from your fingers.

During late fall, your flowerbeds will need an overall tidying up. Try to get to it before the weather is too miserable. Remove annuals, and cut down the herbaceous perennials until they are about 6 to 9 inches above ground level. The stalks are left long to assist in trapping the snow for winter protection, but be sure to remove them first thing the following spring. When pulling up annuals, bang them together gently to shake off the soil so that it stays on the bed where it is most needed. Old plant material can be put straight onto the compost pile.

Late fall is also the time to spend a few hours raking up excess amounts of fallen leaves. Although I have suggested that the annual leaf fall is nature's way of maintaining soil fertility, too many fallen leaves accumulating in the wrong place can be detrimental to plants. Fallen leaves such as those from maples too often lie flat and can smother plants, causing them to rot. Leaves from such trees as the oak do not pack down and are not so bad, but it is a sound policy to remove any leaves that have accumulated on the

41

Shrubs and trees come in all sizes, shapes and colours. A selection that takes into account these elements and shorter plants will result in a garden that works.

crowns of plants and to relegate them to the leaf pile.

It would seem to make sense that a layer of leaves would act as insulation against the cold and so benefit the plants, but in areas of heavy winter snow, that is not the case. If the leaves stayed dry and did not become compacted, some benefits might be felt. Unfortunately, though, small rodents often take up residence among the leaves and then spend the winter digging up and eating the plants beneath. I once mulched a small planting of young red maples in this manner only to lose 80 percent of the trees to meadow voles dining on the bark.

Many of the shade-tolerant herbaceous perennials that are not specific to woodland habitats will, more likely than not, need their main clumps divided every three or four years. When splitting clumps, save the young, vigorous outside pieces for replanting and throw out the weak and often woody central parts.

Some plants, of course, should simply be left where they are. Bleeding heart can stay put almost indefinitely; balloonflower will, in all likelihood, die if you disturb it, and hostas improve in size and beauty the longer you leave them. Naturally, the long-term survival of such plants requires that they are first planted in a deep, well-prepared site.

Plants such as leopard's bane, spotted dead nettle, bergamot, Jacob's ladder, lungwort and globeflower are hard to kill and so are ideal for the rank beginner. Fortunately, they are also very beautiful and well worth a place in any shade garden or perennial border.

Thoughts on Gardens

It is important to remember that different areas of Canada and the northern United States may experience greater or lesser amounts of hot sunshine. As a result, plant species may respond differently from one area to another. One that might perish when exposed to full July sunshine

42

in Ottawa may be quite happy under the same circumstances here in St. John's, Newfoundland. We have found that many plants which are shade-loving elsewhere are, in fact, anything but in our area. It is always an intelligent move to seek advice from successful local gardeners who deal with similar conditions, and it will help to consult one of the more encyclopaedic gardening books at your local library. Such references usually mention whether or not a plant needs shade or sun, while some even provide extensive lists of plants suitable for full or dappled shade. The alternative is to experiment on your own and learn by trial and error like the rest of us. Although it can be somewhat exasperating, experimentation provides the sort of challenge and feeling of adventure that many gardeners relish.

A few well-placed, weathered rocks or perhaps an old log and stump or two improve the woodsy atmosphere of a shade garden. Indeed, plants such as ferns, bloodroot and trilliums simply love being positioned against a rotten log. Rather than struggling to remove a large stump, plant a climber such as Dutchman's pipe, bittersweet or honeysuckle to ramble over it.

A woodland bed should not be planted and maintained in too formal a manner. That would be a contradiction in terms. Instead, it should have a relaxed, more naturalistic character, an effect that is admittedly far easier to create in a larger garden, which can contain plenty of trees and shrubs and where there is space for large clumps of plants and extended sweeps of ground covers, than in a small city lot. Still, I have seen wonderfully transformed shady corners in the heart of large urban centres that are the imaginative exceptions to this rule.

Ground covers such as bugleweed, barrenwort, Japanese spurge and giant rockfoil are all useful in large clumps. Lily-of-the-valley will even do quite well under conifers. Back in the 1950s, when I was a gamekeeper in Lincolnshire, England, we had a 200-acre patch of this tenacious ground cover. A drab green for most of the year, it made a stunning and unforgettable show when in flower.

There are so many lovely garden flowers for all of us to grow and enjoy. While some gardeners in the East may envy the soil and climate of British Columbia or the Niagara Peninsula and even covet some of the plants gardeners on the West Coast can grow, the wonderful thing about gardening is that nature has ensured an unlimited variety of beautiful plants. Regardless of where we live and garden, there are enough to keep us all happily

Lily-of-the-valley is a lush ground cover whose flowers have an unforgettable scent.

scratching in the earth indefinitely. Not only do we have enough herbaceous perennials, biennials and annuals to keep us busy, but there are also bulbs, ferns and shrubs to discover, to grow and to enjoy.

And what of the trees, those huge plants that create garden shade, allowing us to extend our gardening interest to the growing of so varied a mixture of the smaller plants? Think of the trees on your land as a blessing instead of a nuisance. Rather than deterring plant production, they provide a door to the lifelong hobby of gardening in the shade. But be careful: Gardening under trees can become a seductive pastime. Once you engage in it, you will be hooked. Don't get started unless you are willing to spend the rest of your life taking pleasure in it.

Chapter Three:
Shade-Garden Plants

"What will grow in these naturally shaded areas or in those town yards bounded by high walls or in the lee of a high rise?" asks Allen Paterson, director of the Royal Botanical Gardens in Burlington and Hamilton, Ontario, and author of *Plants for Shade and Woodland* (Fitzhenry & Whiteside, 1987). "The answer is lots," he hastens to respond, "lots of the loveliest hardy plants known to man." ⌒ In this final chapter, we get down to the basics of shade gardening: plant selection. Here, five experts from across the continent comment upon their own experience growing dozens of plants that flourish in shade. Since the contributors represent different geographic and climatic regions, gardeners will find it helpful to seek out the comments of the expert who resides in a climatic region similar to their own. We will leave it to the discerning reader to make his or her way through the predictably idiosyncratic preferences expressed by each expert. ⌒ The illustrious members of the panel are: Dianne McLeod (DM), former assistant to the curator at Memorial Botanical Gardens, Memorial University, St. John's, Newfoundland — Agriculture Canada climatic zone 5b; Michael Otis (MO) of the Montreal Botanical Gardens, zone 5b; Lawrence Sherk (LS), horticulturist, Toronto, Ontario, zone 6a; Roger Vick (RV) of the University of Alberta Devonian Botanic Gardens,

Edmonton, Alberta, zone 3a; and Carolyn Jones (CJ), a gardening writer from Burnaby, British Columbia, zone 8b.

Perennials

Aconitum napellus

(monkshood, wolfsbane, helmet flower)

Aconitum is a tall, elegant plant with a long and murky past. It was mentioned by Pliny; barbarian races used it to poison their arrows; and later, so-called civilized folk used it as wolf bait. Legend describes it as the poison Medea put in the cup she prepared for Theseus, and it is said to have been given to the old and infirm on the island of Ceos to speed them on their way to heaven. On the other hand, it is an excellent plant that has been a mainstay in English gardens since before the 10th century, usually without mishap. But the root is lethally poisonous, so it makes sense not to grow it near a food garden, where accidental harvesting becomes a possibility. It is found growing naturally in clumps on shady stream banks and in ditches, pastures and alder groves, but gardeners everywhere argue about

whether it needs sun or shade. I have seen it growing in both sun and shade in a meadow in the Rocky Mountains.

DM: Monkshood is a sturdy perennial for partial shade and moist ground and is tolerant of open and windy sites too. *Aconitum napellus* 'Carneum' shows its best pink flowers in cool shade.

MO: Throughout the garden literature, monkshood is cited as a shade-loving plant, but in our woodland, it needs to be staked and still develops an obvious lean toward the light. There is no doubt it can grow in slightly shaded conditions, but the clumps are sturdier and they bloom better in full sun. New varieties that extend the colour range and flowering period of monkshood are beginning to appear.

LS: The flowers and their colour are a little unusual, but those are the only reasons one might consider growing them.

RV: A good old standby for the cottage garden or herbaceous border. The white-flowered form 'Alba' is sometimes seen, but more popular by far is the purple-and-white-flowered *Aconitum bicolor*.

CJ: This fascinating perennial grows very well on the West Coast and is becoming more readily available. The autumn-blooming *Aconitum carmichaelii*, though somewhat difficult to obtain, is a wonderful sight in September.

Alchemilla mollis

(lady's mantle)

This is a charming foliage plant that forms neat clumps of pleated, grey-green leaves. Overnight dew is collected and held by the leaves, which gives the whole plant a magical appearance. In early summer, it erupts into a froth of enchanting tiny chartreuse flowers. It is at its best when grown in consistently moist soil and partial shade, but it will grow grudgingly in dry areas.

DM: Lady's mantle provides an exotic look and is easy to grow. It suits a wide range of sites with no special requirements. Happily, it enjoys our rains and looks good for it.

MO: Vigorous and easy to grow, with a long period of interest. The flowers are long-lasting, and the foliage, which stays neat and clean for the whole growing season, has its own charm when water drops glisten along the leaf edges. It self-seeds freely and therefore lends itself to naturalized plantings.

LS: This species would seem to be a lightweight entry for the shade garden.

RV: Several species have long been grown in the prairies as foliage plants for shady corners.

CJ: I am very fond of this plant, with its attractive foliage and flowers that are useful for arranging. It seeds itself readily, but unwanted seedlings are easily removed, so it rarely becomes a nuisance. Plants are most attractive in moist, well-drained soil.

Anemone spp

(windflower, anemone)

About 70 species make up this diverse genus, and one can find anemones blooming in spring, summer and fall. Most grow in ordinary garden soil, although they do best in rich, well-drained soil, and all appreciate shelter from the hot afternoon sun and resent being allowed to dry out. They can be propagated from seed, but root division is usually the fastest and most successful method.

Anemone hupehensis

(Chinese anemone)

Found in western China in 1908, this lovely plant is a welcome addition to the fall garden. Well worth looking for are 'Superba' and 'September Charm,' which grow 2½ feet tall and are rather more robust than the species.

DM: The Chinese anemone is known to have grown here over many years. It is a choice plant with soft pink petals, tinged darker beneath. Give it light shade and moist but well-drained soil.

MO: The number of shade plants that bloom in the fall is quite meagre, and this feature alone makes the Chinese anemone worthwhile. It spreads quickly by means of underground stolons and seems hardier than the Japanese anemone. The soft pink flowers carried on long stems could be enhanced by a careful siting against a background of dark-needled conifers.

LS: Can't get too excited about any of the anemones.

RV: A single group of this species, established in 1983 from seed obtained from the Shanghai Botanical Garden, has done well for the past seven years. However, seed of the same species from Germany failed to overwinter, so hardiness appears to be variable depending upon seed source. Once established, its late-August flowers and large compound leaves are distinctive enough to win the Chinese anemone a place in more prairie gardens.

CJ: These fall-blooming anemones are very easy to grow and well liked because of their cheerful flowers late in the season. They tend to run a bit in the garden but seem easy to control.

Aquilegia spp

(columbine, granny's bonnet, dancing fairies)

Dancing fairies aptly describes these delightful flowers of the early-summer garden. The dainty, many-hued blooms are balanced on slender stems high above a mound of blue-green leaves and are set dancing by the slightest breeze. They are easy to grow from seed, but a long taproot makes it imperative that you plant seedlings in their permanent position when they are small. A garden is not complete without some.

DM: Individual plants are not long-lived but "move about," seeding throughout the garden and filling gaps here and there. Transplant only when small, but otherwise, columbine survives considerable shade and neglect. The foliage alone is pleasant, and the lovely shades of spurred flowers are an added bonus.

MO: *Aquilegia vulgaris* will grow well and flower profusely in shady places. Our native columbine, *A. canadensis*, will do better in lightly shaded locations. Allow some seedlings to grow around the plants, because individual plants are short-lived but self-sow freely.

LS: Even after all these years, it is pretty hard to beat 'McKanna Giant' for aristocratic flowers.

RV: Short-lived, but often self-seeding. The species that have stayed with us longest are *Aquilegia alpina* (blue/purple), *A. canadensis* (red/yellow), *A. caerulea* (blue/white), *A. flabellata* (purple/lilac), *A. flavescens* (yellow), *A. formosa* (red/yellow), *A. viridiflora* (green/brown) and *A. vulgaris* (many colours). Two good cultivars are 'McKanna Giant' and 'Nora Barlow.'

CJ: Many species and hybrids of columbine are available on the West Coast, and they are easy to grow from seed. The only problem they have is leaf miners.

Arisaema spp

(Jack-in-the-pulpit)

A wildflower of our eastern woodlands, Jack-in-the-pulpit has the most intriguing flowers, which are followed by spectacular clusters of bright orange fruits. Moist, shady conditions suit it. The root is a corm resembling that of the gladiolus and was used for food by native Americans. It is sometimes called Indian turnip but is only edible after it has been processed to remove the toxic compound calcium oxalate. Please do not dig plants found in the wild. It is easily propagated from seed, planted half an inch deep where it is to grow or in flats that are left outside for the winter.

DM: In medium to dark conditions, the pouch-shaped flowers of these unusual plants will produce orange-red fruits.

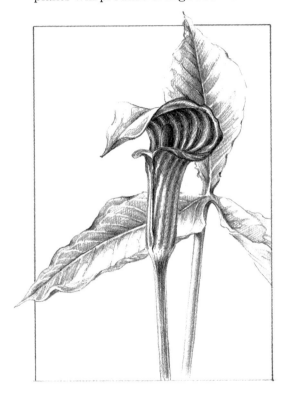

MO: One of our most commonly grown wildflowers. Check that stock is nursery-propagated and not collected from the wild before buying. Once established, it will produce a lot of offsets that can be separated to increase your planting. Although easygoing, they need constant moisture; otherwise, they disappear from the garden scene early in the season. Some exotic-looking Japanese species are available, but these are best left to the experienced gardener.

LS: Jack-in-the-pulpit never fails to create interest for the moist, shady garden.

RV: *Arisaema japonicum* and *A. triphyllum* are satisfactory around Edmonton.

CJ: A successful plant in the Vancouver area but very hard to get. More of a collector's item.

Astilbe hybrids

(astilbe, false spiraea)

Astilbes are excellent plants for shady, moist conditions, with over 20 species, from 2 inches to 4 feet in height, and many more hybrids. Flowering from June to mid-August, they range in colour from white to blood-red, and foliage varies from copper to dark green. Dryness is their worst enemy; it causes foliage to develop brown margins and even whole leaves to wither and die early. Propagate by division in spring or fall.

DM: Astilbes are reliable and showy in leaf and in flower. Taller varieties will take anywhere from 30 to 60 percent sun. *Astilbe chinensis pumila* forms a leafy carpet with spikes of purple-pink blooms and is easily grown in dappled sun or considerable shade.

MO: These are favourite old standbys, with so many cultivars available that choosing a few becomes difficult. *Astilbe taquetii* 'Superba,' one of the last to bloom with nice purplish panicles carried on long 49

stems, will tolerate slightly drier conditions than most.

LS: These are great for moist, shaded areas. I particularly like the reds and pinks, although the white can be used to provide contrast.

RV: These are some of the more colourful plants for the shady border. The better ones at the botanic garden are 'Bonn,' 'Bridal Veil,' 'Deutschland,' 'Diamond,' 'Irrlicht,' 'Ostrich Plume,' 'Peach Blossom,' 'Pink Pearl' and 'Spartan.'

CJ: Must-have plants for the shady garden. The many German hybrids are very popular. The small *Astilbe chinensis pumila* and the tall *A. taquetii* 'Superba' are also grown here.

Campanula spp

(bellflower)

In bellflowers, we have an astonishing array of good ornamentals ranging from stately border plants to small rock-garden specimens. Most are well-behaved, but a few are garden thugs, so care must be taken. *Campanula rapunculoides*, for instance, should only be introduced into the wildest part of your garden. In a well-ordered border, it becomes an ineradicable, if beautiful, weed, which spreads aggressively by rhizomes. Most campanulas are easily propagated by seed, cuttings or root division.

DM: Among the shade-tolerant species long grown in Newfoundland are *Campanula glomerata*, *C. persicifolia* and *C. rapunculoides*. They will reward the most negligent gardener with perfect bells in shades of deep purple to white. New and notable in our trials is *C. lactiflora*.

MO: *Campanula cochlearifolia* and *C. carpatica* could probably put on a decent display in shade.

LS: I can't say I have ever used these or seen any of them growing in shaded areas.

RV: There must be a campanula for everyone. I use *Campanula carpatica* alone down a border shaded by a fence on one side and a house on the other, and it flowers from midsummer until covered by

winter snow. Self-seeding, it is also useful in the meadow garden, together with *C. rotundifolia*. I am especially fond of the dainty species, such as *C. cochlearifolia*.

CJ: This popular genus is well represented here. The four most widely cultivated species are peach-leaf bellflower (*Campanula persicifolia*), clustered bellflower (*C. glomerata*), Carpathian harebell (*C. carpatica*) – especially 'Blue Clips' and 'White Clips' – and the spreaders such as *C. portenschlagiana* and its hybrids.

Convallaria majalis

(lily-of-the-valley)

This favourite fragrant plant makes a fine if rampant ground cover when happy, but where conditions are not to its liking, it will sit in a sulk. Still, the common lily-of-the-valley is worth growing well. Cultivars available are 'Fortin's Giant,' which is 12 to 15 inches tall with ¾-inch-long flowers; *Convallaria majalis* 'Flore Pleno,' with cream-coloured double flowers; *C. m. striata*, with variegated green-and-white-striped leaves and white flowers; and *C. m. rosea*, which is described as having light pink flowers, although in my garden, they are a dingy-looking muddy pink.

DM: Lily-of-the-valley produces the sweetest perfume of all shade-garden

graceful foliage topped by pink or white heart-shaped flowers. Several are native to North America, but plants of the common bleeding heart (*D. spectabilis*) were first introduced to England from Japan by Robert Fortune in the 1840s. The flowers of this one in particular look for all the world like tiny pairs of pantaloons hanging on a clothesline, hence the alternative common name. Grow in rich, moist but well-drained soil. Bleeding heart can be raised from seed sown in flats and left outside under snow for the winter, or plants can be divided, preferably in early spring.

DM: *Dicentra spectabilis* is a must-have. If given a well-prepared soil with ample organic matter, clumps will continue to expand for years. Because of our cool growing season, these plants can reach a height of 4 to 5 feet and bloom well into August. Semishade is ideal, but much more is tolerated. *D. formosa* and *D. eximia* are also worthwhile for their lasting bloom and ease of care. These smaller species have more delicate, divided foliage.

MO: The traditional bleeding heart and its lovely white version can grace shady corners until October. They are known to wilt and go dormant if the soil is permitted to dry out during the summer, but with ample moisture, the mound of foliage will

plants. Grow in moist, organic soil where the rhizomes can spread out freely.

MO: The scent is sufficient reason to plant it, and with time, it can make a nice low-maintenance ground cover.

LS: An old-fashioned favourite that can become invasive if left to its own devices. Hard to beat the fragrance of the flowers.

RV: Reliably hardy and found in shade gardens everywhere. However, because it is rarely lifted and replanted in rich organic soil (as it should be in order to produce flowers), it frequently looks as jaded as a dusty aspidistra. There are many alternative shade plants that are more interesting and much less trouble.

CJ: An old-fashioned flower, lily-of-the-valley grows very well here, even in dry shade where few other plants flourish.

Dicentra spp

(bleeding heart, Dutchman's breeches)

The different species of *Dicentra* vary in height from 1 to 3 feet, but most have

stay in good shape until September and then turn a pale yellow with the arrival of frost. The smaller dicentras bloom on and off all summer, with *Dicentra* 'Luxuriant,' *D. eximia* and its white form *D. e. alba* being good choices.

LS: Another old favourite, particularly *Dicentra spectabilis*. The lower-growing species provide interest too. I like the cultivar 'Luxuriant,' which still had a flower one November 1 in my garden.

RV: Every cottage garden must have its bleeding heart. Once established, they usually prove surprisingly enduring, although the white-flowered form is less so. Rather less reliable on the prairies are *D. eximia* and *D. formosa*.

CJ: The common bleeding heart is popular and is easy both to get and to grow. Its biggest drawback is that it dies down in summer. An excellent bleeding heart is the hybrid 'Luxuriant,' which has beautiful foliage and blooms from May until frost. Fringed bleeding heart (*D. eximia*) and Pacific bleeding heart (*D. formosa*), both native to Canada, are attractive but perhaps a bit invasive for some settings.

Epimedium spp

(barrenwort)

Long-lived and adaptable, barrenworts form wonderful clumps of compound foliage and unusual small hooded or spurred flowers held in airy sprays; but they are slow to become established. In spring, the leaves are often tinged pink or red, and in the fall, they may turn yellow, red or bronze. The flowers can be seen and appreciated better if the old foliage is clipped close to the ground in early spring. These plants look their best when grown in good moist soil. They can, however, compete with tree roots and tolerate heavy shade, growing in barren places where other plants fade away. Propagate by division in late summer.

DM: From tough mats of rhizomes arise stalked, heart-shaped leaves. This foliage is useful for softening edges or framing the base of a birch or cherry tree. The rather delicate flowers vary from cream to yellow to ruby-red. Perfectly hardy are *Epimedium alpinum*, *E. grandiflorum* and *E. rubrum*.

MO: With time, all make perfect ground covers with pretty columbinelike flowers and nice leaves that take on copper and reddish hues in the fall and stay in good condition until the first snowfall. The yellow-flowered species like *Epimedium perralderianum* seem to be less hardy than other types and would benefit from a mulch of leaves in the fall.

LS: A real wildflower or woodland plant that needs good woodsy soil to establish itself and persist.

RV: Of several species tried, *Epimedium rubrum* and *E. youngianum* 'Niveum' have proved to be the most satisfactory.

CJ: Lovely plants that should be more widely grown. Perhaps they are overshadowed by showier perennials.

Galium odoratum

(sweet woodruff)

Sprigs of sweet woodruff (also listed as *Asperula odorata*) are essential for the making of May wine, and in Germany, spring would not be complete without it. The same can be said for the shade garden. Narrow green leaves grow in starlike whorls topped by clusters of tiny white funnel-shaped flowers in early summer. Once valued as a strewing herb, woodruff is still useful for scenting linen cupboards with a delightful mix of hay, honey and vanilla. This plant is slightly fragrant in the garden, but it becomes far more aromatic as it dries. Although it is easiest to start with plants, sweet woodruff can also be grown from seed sown in the fall, but germination is slow. Once established, it will self-seed.

DM: This herb is easily grown and enjoys moist ground and moderate shade.

MO: It ranks on top of the list of ground covers for shade. The whorled leaves stay nice and neat late into the fall, and the small creamy flowers give it character. Maintenance-free, it deserves to be used more liberally.

LS: Sweet woodruff has a nice fine texture, almost misty when in flower. It is great for massing.

RV: This species is not grown in the botanic garden. Five other species of *Asperula*, however, are well established.

CJ: Pretty and easy to grow, but very invasive and must be planted with care. It looks attractive growing with bugleweed (*Ajuga reptans*) – the blue spires and white

stars combine well, and the plants seem equally vigorous.

Geranium spp

(cranesbill)

Known as cranesbill because of the beaklike seed head, this diverse genus is not to be confused with the popular bedding plant known by the common name geranium. Thriving in any average soil, there is a geranium to suit almost every situation. Plants range from low mats and neat clumps to tall upright plants or straggly clumps needing the support of a few twiggy pea sticks; but all are attractive in both leaf and flower. Propagate by division in spring or fall; by cuttings taken in the spring or after flowering; or from seed.

DM: The medium-height blue- or white-flowering *Geranium pratense* is easily grown but best if in only light shade. Good clump-forming perennials for moderate shade are *G. sanguineum* and the scented-leafed *G. macrorrhizum*.

MO: There is a perennial geranium for almost every situation, and all are easy to grow, hardy and very welcome additions in shade. *Geranium macrorrhizum* rapidly

53

covers large patches of ground in shady nooks with aromatic leaves. *G. maculatum*, with lilac-coloured blooms in late spring, suits the wildflower garden. *G. phaeum* is known for its dark flowers, a purple shade close to black, and for its ability to thrive in heavy shade.

LS: Geraniums always provide a good show of colour.

RV: The horizontal leaves and slowly spreading root system of *Geranium macrorrhizum* make it a good ground cover. The usually magenta flowers are of secondary importance, although those of 'Ingwersen's Variety' are an attractive pale pink.

CJ: Cranesbills have taken off in popularity here in the past five years. They do well in dry shade, and some bloom almost all summer. There are many species and cultivars available, more each year.

Hemerocallis hybrids

(day lily)

Few perennials are as universally popular as day lilies, with their stout stems holding clusters of gorgeous lilylike flowers high above straplike, bright green,

arching foliage. Along with the common lilac, older types are often found marking the site of some long-abandoned homestead, while newer varieties have become the mainstay of commercial plantings around public buildings, parks and condominiums. Chinese cooks consider the buds and dried flowers a special table delicacy, but all parts of the plant are edible. Lewis Hill, in his new book *Daylilies*, says that over 32,000 day lilies have been named, enough choice for even the most discriminating gardener.

DM: Even in gardens where there is very little sun, day lilies will flourish and bloom. There are so many colours to choose from: yellows, oranges, bronze and mixes, in addition to the new hybrids that come in shades of pink. Some are early, some later, and many are fragrant. We grow old strains of *Hemerocallis citrina*, *H. flava* and *H. fulva*, as well as new selections such as 'Chicago Raspberry' and 'Stella d'Oro.'

MO: We haven't experimented with day lilies in our shade garden, but I am sure they could bloom satisfactorily in these conditions with a few hours of sunlight a day.

LS: It is hard to find a group of plants more versatile than the day lilies. Sun or shade, woodland, streamside, you name it, they thrive there. Dig them up, split them up, pass them on. Nurseries would possibly go out of business if all plants were as easy to grow.

RV: Day lilies are virtually indestructible, so much so that they can be moved around the garden anytime that the soil is not frozen. They surely have a great future as plant breeders continue to select for improved flower-colour combinations and length of blooming season. Be aware, however, that evergreen types are being bred for entirely different climatic zones than ours, and these will not necessarily do well in the Prairie Provinces.

CJ: Although well liked on the West Coast, day lilies are not as popular here as I understand they are in the East. They are healthy and easy to grow, but most

54

gardeners only allow space for one or two. They are usually grown in full sun.

Hosta spp and hybrids

(plantain lily, hosta)

After lying around neglected for centuries, hostas have, over the last 20 years or so, suddenly exploded into well-earned popularity and become the darlings of North American gardeners. Few plants can do more for a shade garden. They vary in size from 6-inch-tall plants suitable for edging paths to huge, stately specimens making their own architectural statement. Leaves display a broad range of textures, shapes and colours. They can be puckered, ridged or smooth; shiny or glaucous with a waxy bloom; round, heart-shaped or pointed and slim. Leaf colour varies from light to dark green, yellow-green or blue-green, and many have margins or central variegations in white, cream or yellow. The flowers, which are considered of only secondary importance, are splendid spires of lilac, purple or white blooms, with an added bonus of fragrance in some varieties.

Plants can be divided in early spring. They do, however, age with dignity, growing more handsome each year, and should be left alone unless more stock is required. Mulching around the crowns with grit will help to cut down on slug and snail damage.

DM: Hostas do very well in our area. I would not be without them.

MO: The wealth of hostas available makes a choice difficult. All are tough and durable shade plants with good ornamental value. They are one of the rare plants that can survive in the heavy shade and despite the competing roots of trees such as silver maples.

LS: Hard to beat for their bold foliage effect. Nice to see that many more cultivars are becoming readily available. Summer flowers always provide an extra dividend. This is the plant I recommend for that narrow border between the sidewalk and the side of the house, an area that usually receives very little sun.

RV: A welcome diversion in any herbaceous border, doing particularly well in rich but well-drained soils. In my view, the flowers are of less consequence than the textured or colourful foliage. Good ones at the botanic garden include *Hosta lancifolia, H. sieboldiana, H. fortunei aureomarginata, H. f. hyacinthina* and *H. undulata albomarginata.*

CJ: Hostas are number one for a moist, shady garden. There are so many to choose from, and all seem to do equally well. Some favourites here are 'Frances Williams,' with its huge variegated leaves; 'Royal Standard,' with gardenia-scented flowers late in the summer; 'August Moon' and other gold-leafed cultivars; all of the green-and-white cultivars; and the lovely blues, such as *Hosta sieboldiana elegans.*

Monarda hybrids

(bergamot, bee balm, Oswego tea)

John Bartram first collected bee balm near Oswego, New York, on Lake On-

prompted me to forget them in the woodland garden. Nevertheless, if there is good air circulation around the plants, they would be satisfactory in light shade.

LS: Colourful and useful because of the variety of shades that are available today. The new hybrids are quite floriferous.

RV: We have been very successful occasionally with the bright red-flowered *Monarda didyma* 'Cambridge Scarlet.' *M. fistulosa* selections are more permanent but less impressive. All tend to die out from the centre, thus demanding frequent division and transplanting.

CJ: Popular and readily available border perennials. They are lovely for attracting butterflies.

Polygonatum multiflorum

(Solomon's seal)

An elegant woodlander with long, gracefully arching, unbranched stems bearing alternate leaves and creamy-white, pendulous flowers hanging from the leaf nodes. It can grow 3 to 4 feet tall in shady, moist areas and will tolerate heavy shade. Once established, it will even do quite well in dry conditions. There is considerable confusion and disagreement on the correct naming of these plants, but a variegated form with cream stripes on the foliage is well worth looking for.

DM: A heritage plant from old Newfoundland gardens. This gracious perennial, with its beautiful arching stems, prefers the cool morning sun and a rich organic soil or streamside setting. Since it must be supported against our strong winds, the easiest technique is to place alder branches upright between the emerging shoots. The foliage of Solomon's seal will quickly conceal the supporting twigs.

MO: Solomon's seal increases slowly, but the quality of the foliage and the green-tipped white flowers are worth the wait. It will thrive in any kind of shade as long as moisture is available at its feet.

RV: The small hanging flowers are interesting, but once the novelty has worn off, this coarse plant is of little ornamen-

tario, and early pioneers learned from the native population how to use it, but the name *Monarda* commemorates Nicholas Monardes, a Spanish physician who discovered the plant's properties in the 16th century. There are some good named hybrids, ranging from 2 to 4 feet tall in colours from white through pink and red to purplish violet. Moist soil and partial shade suit them best, but they are tolerant of less than perfect conditions. They are very good for attracting bees, butterflies and hummingbirds.

DM: From the start of the season, with the scent of aromatic foliage, to blooming time, this member of the mint family is easy and rewarding in our moist, cool climate. The species *Monarda fistulosa*, with its soft lilac flowers, and hybrids of *M. didyma*, such as 'Cambridge Scarlet,' have been long-lasting. They appreciate regular division every three years or so, to rejuvenate the clumps, and prefer filtered light or afternoon shade.

MO: A tendency for monardas to be afflicted with powdery mildew in bad years

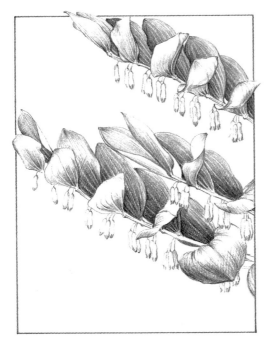

a dramatic spring floral display before any leaves appear, especially when it is planted en masse. To increase their numbers, simply divide after flowering, before the heat of summer sets in. *Primula denticulata cachmeriana* has been the source of some of the best forms I have seen. They are happiest grown in dappled shade under a deciduous canopy where the air is humid.

MO: One of the first perennials to bloom. It asks only that you provide a steady supply of water at its feet, and it will prove very useful along streamsides. The large floppy leaves that follow the short-stemmed flowers remind me of Chinese lettuce. I have learned to plant this one toward the back of beds and borders.

LS: One of my favourites and a winner as long as its demanding requirements are satisfied.

Primula japonica

(Japanese primrose)

Primula japonica is another lovely primrose that likes wet feet. A massed planting beside a stream with gently moving water will make a spectacular display. Given wet soil, this is one of the easiest of the candelabra-type primroses to grow. Flower heads, in colours ranging from white and pale pinks to crimsons and purplish reds, are held high above the foliage. The head is made up of 2 to 6 whorls, each consisting of 8 to 12 flowers nearly an inch across and held at right angles to the stem. Easily grown from seed, it can also be propagated by division.

DM: This species is a water lover and will enjoy streamside planting or moist ground. To maintain lasting, rich-coloured flowers, grow without direct sunlight in medium shade.

MO: These extend the blooming period into June and are among the easiest primroses to grow. Will do well in shade or sun provided their moisture requirements are met. Glorious sight when planted en masse along ponds and streams.

LS: Makes one think of some of the

tal value. It is best suited to the wild garden, where it will persist without becoming invasive.

CJ: Only readily available at club sales, but an outstanding perennial for our area and one of my favourites. Pest- and disease-free, it thrives in sun or shade, damp soil or dry. The foliage looks good all summer and turns yellow in the fall. And then, of course, there are the lovely flowers.

Primula denticulata

(drumstick primrose)

This popular native of the Himalayas is happiest in the bog garden, by a stream or in a moist border, but I have had it do quite well in an average shaded border. Large globular heads of purple, pink, mauve or white blooms are held aloft on strong stems above newly emerging foliage in early spring. Luxuriant growth of long, broad, coarse leaves follows flowering. Easily grown from seed, the seedlings flower the second year, but the quality of seed-grown plants is variable. Any good forms that emerge should be increased by root cuttings.

DM: The drumstick primrose puts on

great British gardens. Definitely does not like hot, dry summers.

Primula polyantha

(polyanthus)

Polyanthuses are used as standard spring bedding plants in the gentle climate of England, but in most parts of Canada, they are not the easiest of primulas to grow. The glorious array of new colours available, however, has made them the darlings of the greenhouse pot-plant trade, which in turn makes them readily obtainable. After enjoying the flowers indoors, plant them in a cool, shady spot with humusy, moisture-retentive soil.

DM: There are some old forms that have been in Newfoundland gardens for years, but many of the new varieties are not as tolerant of frost heave unless special care is taken to prepare a moist but well-drained organic mix. Light shade is best. Keep out of hot midday sun, or heat stress will leave these plants prone to aphids and mites.

MO: Will survive in areas of the garden where snow lies longest. Planting where the snow disappears quickly in the spring, while night temperatures can still go down occasionally to minus 4 degrees F, will most likely kill them. *Primula elatior* and *P. veris* have proved hardier, blooming at about the same time.

LS: Would that it were easy to grow here in southern Ontario. Certainly does make a beautiful pot plant.

Primula sieboldii

(Siebold's primrose)

A personal favourite, Siebold's primrose has 6-to-8-inch-high umbels of rounded white, pink, blue-mauve or purple blooms massed above light green, heart-shaped leaves with scalloped margins. There are also some with prettily fringed flowers. The plants tend to go dormant after flowering, especially if the soil gets dry. I like to grow them in a mixed planting with tiarella, which fills the gap and prevents

the primulas from being accidentally disturbed. Easily grown from seed or careful division in early spring.

DM: *Primula sieboldii* requires medium shade and damp organic soil that remains moist yet well-drained. Very beautiful.

MO: Maybe its habit of disappearing quickly after blooming until the following spring has led to its scarcity in the trade. It is easy to grow and worth a search.

LS: Another great one for the moist, shaded garden.

RV: For 30 years, all the primulas have been very satisfactory in moist organic soil here at the Devonian Botanic Garden.

CJ: All of the primroses do very well on the West Coast. The showy polyanthuses, sold everywhere in fall and early spring, are not terribly perennial, but the rest of them are, provided they do not dry out too much in summer.

Sanguinaria canadensis

(bloodroot)

The common and scientific names refer to sanguinarine, a red-coloured toxic alkaloid sap found in the roots and rhizomes of bloodroot. Despite its toxicity, the sap has long been used with oak bark to make a red dye. Thick shoots push through the ground in early spring. At this stage, the leaf is wrapped tightly around the flower bud. As it begins to unfurl, the flower bud grows straight up and the single, rounded, 4-to-8-inch-wide, pale green leaf opens. Bloodroots will grow in dense shade, provided they have sun in early spring when they do most of their growing. Moisture-retentive, humus-rich soil in light shade is probably ideal, and in such conditions, they will spread rapidly. They are easily propagated from rhizome division when the leaves have just finished yellowing. Wear gloves and wash your hands well after handling the rhizomes.

DM: The single-flowered species and the double white *Sanguinaria canadensis multiplex* have been grown in Newfoundland for a number of years. Prepare moist, organic soil with adequate drainage, and set in light shade.

MO: A harbinger of spring, the blood-root should be planted where you will not miss its ephemeral floral display.

LS: A great native wildflower. The double-flowered *S. c. multiplex* is the best bet, the blooms lasting much longer than those of the single, which may only flower for a day or two if the weather turns hot.

RV: A choice plant for the shady wild garden, where it is one of the earliest flowers to bloom.

CJ: Connoisseurs on the West Coast grow bloodroots — single, double and a pink-budded form — and say they do beautifully. They like damp soil and die back in early summer. I hope that they become better known.

Thalictrum spp

(meadow-rue)

Dainty yet stately plants with ferny foliage and delicate powder puffs of flowers, the meadow-rues are among the most graceful of garden plants. The ancient Romans believed that laying a newborn baby on a pillow of thalictrum flowers would ensure it riches throughout its life. Light shade and ordinary soil suit them well enough, but they will enjoy some moisture-holding organic matter worked in. Grow them lean rather than well-fed, since overfertilizing promotes weak growth. They are propagated by division or seed.

DM: *Thalictrum adiantifolium*, a heritage plant found in old Newfoundland gardens, is recommended for the attractiveness of its foliage. It is easy to cultivate in light to medium shade. The taller *T. delavayi* 'Hewitt's Double' has delightful rosy-lilac flower sprays. Although slow to become established, it is one of the interesting new plants now available locally.

MO: A small sampling of meadow-rues allows you to enjoy their fluffy blooms for a few months. *Thalictrum aquilegifolium*, which blooms in spring, is easy to please and readily available. *T. delavayi* 'Hewitt's Double' reminds me of a lilac gypsophila; it needs staking and a mulch of leaves for winter protection in the fall. *T. rochebrunianum*, which is more difficult to obtain,

them highly organic, moisture-retentive soil in medium to heavy shade. I have grown them in dryish soil in light shade, but they struggled rather than thrived. Propagate by seed or division.

DM: This species is not found in gardens in Newfoundland, but many of its closest relatives do well for us. It is likely to succeed in light to medium shade or a morning-sun spot.

MO: This native wildflower should be seen more often in our gardens. No pests bother it, and it spreads freely. The hazy cloud of white flowers will lighten the garden year after year. If you prefer a non-spreader, *Tiarella wherryi* is clump-forming and has pinkish flowers and leaves spotted with brown.

is of the same colour, but the sepals are larger and showier.

LS: This is really delicate and a must for the shaded woodland garden.

RV: Worth growing for the fine "maidenhair fern" type of foliage. Species vary remarkably in stature and showiness of flower. *Thalictrum minus* can be so dwarf as to be of value only in an alpine garden, while *T. rochebrunianum*, admittedly short-lived, has reached heights of 7 feet in moist shade. Try *T. aquilegifolium* selections for flower colour.

CJ: All species and cultivars of meadow-rue do well here. Although not easy to get, the species can be grown from seed available from the Alpine Garden Club.

Tiarella cordifolia

(foamflower)

Charming woodland plants that form mounds of heart-shaped, three-to-five-lobed leaves. The evergreen foliage shows burgundy markings in the spring and fall, but in winter, it often turns completely bronze in areas where it is not covered by snow. It is spring-flowering, with pink-tinged flower buds opening into dainty racemes of creamy white stars. Flowering usually lasts for about six weeks. Give

LS: A great ground cover for moist, shaded areas with rich organic soils. It will not tolerate drying out.

RV: Reminiscent of *Heuchera*, *Tiarella* is most suited to the wild garden, where its fall foliage colour can be quite attractive. Survives well but does not increase.

CJ: Not widely grown on the West Coast, but I'm sure it would do very well. Our native species is *Tiarella trifoliata*, which is not often cultivated either.

Viola spp

(violet, Johnny-jump-up)

A large number of violets will thrive in shaded areas. Most of these are perennial, some surviving for only a few years, but if they are happy, they will self-seed freely – so freely, in fact, that they can become invasive weeds. Violets come in a range of colours, not only violet but also white, yellow and blue. All like a damp soil rich in humus. The annual pansies are hybrids that may have some of the following species in their makeup.

DM: Violets enjoy moist, humid sites and will flower even in considerable shade. We grow *Viola adunca*, *V. odorata*, *V. palustris* and *V. tricolor*.

MO: *Viola odorata* and its many colour variants make spectacular carpets among shrubs or anywhere in shade. They cope well with dense shade and short spells of drought and are weed-proof. *V. canaden-*

sis is worth growing for its long flowering period.

LS: Native violets can easily take over, so they must be used with care.

RV: Somewhat ephemeral plants but well suited to the shade garden. *Viola cornuta* is a countrified charmer, while selections like 'Arkwright's Ruby' have flower size and colour that take them into the big league. Large-flowered cultivars are likely to be short-lived, while the small-flowered kinds, like *V. tricolor*, are so prolific that they are best restricted to the meadow garden.

CJ: The violet grown by most gardeners is the sweet violet (*Viola odorata*), and it does very well here. Alpine enthusiasts collect other species such as *V. labradorica*, which has bronzy foliage.

Annuals

Begonia semperflorens

(wax begonia)

This South American perennial is grown here as a tender annual. Usually in bloom at the time of purchase, it will continue to flower profusely until killed by frost. Fo-

61

liage colour varies from glossy bright green to a dark bronzy shade. A green-and-white variegated type, which I find most unattractive, is occasionally available. Flowers are white, pink or red, and the plants grow 8 to 12 inches tall.

DM: An easy plant for dappled or medium shade, providing strong colour in a moist, cool setting.

MO: Wax begonias are among the easiest annuals to accommodate in shade. They grow and bloom profusely no matter what the soil or the degree of light.

LS: Wax begonias are great in filtered sun or deep shade. Too bad the colours are not a little more interesting.

RV: A staple of annual shade plantings.

CJ: An outstanding bedding plant for the climate in Vancouver. They bloom from May until frost. If potted up and taken indoors, they will continue right through to the next spring and happily go out to the garden again. Cutworms can be a problem.

Coleus hybrids

(coleus, painted nettle)

A flamboyant member of the mint family, coleus is grown for its multicoloured foliage. It will send up spikes of blue flowers, but they should be cut off as they appear to encourage foliar growth. There are hundreds of cultivars, varying in size from 6 to 36 inches, in a wide range of colour combinations and leaf shapes. When buying, decide what size plant you need, then look for foliage that pleases you.

DM: Generally speaking, foliage plants become lush in our moist growing season. Provide light to medium shade in order to get rich leaf colours.

MO: An excellent foliage plant. Can be disappointing in deep shade, where it shows lanky growth and poor colours. The 'Saber' series is a good compact strain.

LS: Great for shade. The foliage provides good colour contrast to the various flowering annuals.

RV: This seems to need a cooler summer than we are able to provide. Mine produce unwanted flower spikes but little good foliage growth.

CJ: Coleus is an attractive bedding plant for shady places, especially useful in large pots and window boxes.

Digitalis purpurea

(common foxglove)

This old-time favourite of cottage gardens is enjoying a return to popularity. They are erect plants with alternate leaves usually crowded at the base in an attractive rosette but becoming sparser up the stem. The tall, often one-sided spikes of bell-shaped flowers are commonly in shades of purple, yellow or white. 'Foxy,' which grows 2½ feet tall, and the 5-foot 'Excelsior' hybrids are readily available. Some of the species are very garden-worthy and easy to grow from seed, if you can find them.

DM: For ease and high impact, the biennial *Digitalis purpurea* puts on a splendid show each year, especially when allowed to grow en masse in a shaded glade. The new annual cultivars, such as 'Foxy,' are only recently being tried.

MO: Montreal snow cover is not dependable enough for most of the biennial strains to be big performers. 'Foxy' is an

when buying. The colour range is wide, with shadings of red, pink, orange, salmon, purple, white and almost any combination of these. They prefer moist soils.

DM: This species likes the cool of light to deep shade. Use it to brighten the understorey where other annuals will not bloom.

MO: Impatiens is a good reliable annual for shade and a most welcome filler for us. It can grow and put on a reasonable show in amazingly dark corners, provided the soil is moist.

LS: No shaded garden can be without them, although they do tend to take over to the exclusion of other annuals.

exception. This strain will bloom the first year from seed. For something different, the rusty foxglove (*Digitalis ferruginea*) brings strong vertical lines to the garden with its tall, tapered spikes of buff-coloured flowers and a glossy rosette of symmetrically arranged leaves. It self-sows abundantly, thus providing plants for years to come.

RV: Well worth trying. The cultivar 'Foxy' is very good in sun or shade.

CJ: Handsome and useful plants where height is needed in a sunny or shady spot. Some gardeners frown on them because they are common, but I always welcome a few seedlings each year.

Impatiens wallerana

(impatiens, busy Lizzie, patience plant)

Busy Lizzie is the queen of annuals in the shade garden, for nothing else gives quite such an extensive block of summer-long colour. The plants are rather brittle and easily damaged during handling but are very forgiving; once planted, they quickly grow into mounds of solid bloom. There are many hybrids available, with heights from 6 to 36 inches, so do check labels

RV: Busy Lizzie gives continuous bloom in shade. I prefer the hefty tall kinds, as they are more thrifty than many of the modern namby-pamby miniatures. The policeman's helmet, or tree orchid (*Impatiens glandulifera*), is the latest local fad for shady corners. Dozens of volunteer seedlings appear wherever a plant went to seed the previous season, and the few that are allowed to remain quickly grow 6 to 10 feet in height. The adequate and substantial flowers are usually pink, sometimes white. Thick-stemmed and shallow- 63 rooted, the plant needs to be staked against sudden storms.

CJ: Impatiens is the number-one bedding plant for the shady garden. It blooms from May to frost.

Lobelia erinus

(lobelia)

Lobelia prefers cool conditions but will do well even in hot and humid areas if given shade and moisture. Growing only 3 to 8 inches high, it is most often a deep blue colour, but white, pale blue and red shades, some with a white eye, are becoming increasingly popular. Foliage can be bright green or a very dark, almost bluish green. Erect growers for the garden and trailing types for hanging baskets and planters are available.

DM: This will provide reliable, rich blue colour for containers or walls in light, medium or partially shaded areas.

MO: Welcome as one of the few blue annuals for shade. 'Blue Butterflies' is noteworthy, having flowers twice the size of other varieties. A little shearing may be beneficial if plants stop blooming after extended periods of heat and drought.

LS: Great at the front of the border or in hanging baskets.

RV: Consistently satisfactory in shade. The trailing cultivar 'Pendula' is particularly attractive in hanging baskets.

CJ: This annual is used by the mile to edge shady borders in our area. It blooms all summer, and its bright blue flowers combine well with many other bedding plants. Lobelia is grown extensively in hanging baskets and window boxes.

Myosotis sylvatica

(forget-me-not)

Of forget-me-nots, William Robinson, a famous 19th-century gardening journalist, wrote: "A beautiful woodland plant and of great value for the wild garden. It should be abundant in a wild state by wood walks [and] in copses and sows itself freely in such places." I garden on a smaller scale but enjoy seeing my shrubs awash in a sea of blue every spring. Plants self-seed with reckless abandon but are easily controlled. I often allow volunteers to flower for a time and rip them out as they begin to interfere with choicer plants. White and pink forms are available, but they will revert to blue unless grown in isolation or rogue blues are ruthlessly removed.

DM: One of the simple joys early in the season is picking a bouquet of forget-me-nots. I would always have room for these easy plants. Tight clumps full of flowers are produced in open sites. Without direct sunlight, the plants become more upright and loose and give a pleasant lacy effect. Allow some to self-seed, and they will endure without care.

MO: A good biennial that looks its best naturalized with daffodils. If it were not prone to attack by powdery mildew during muggy summers, it would be perfect.

RV: Forget it.

CJ: Once this is in your garden, you won't be able to forget it. It seeds itself everywhere but can easily be pulled up where it is not wanted. It is so bright and cheery, however, that it is hard to resist.

Nicotiana alata

(flowering tobacco)

Old types tend to droop during the day but open in the evening to fill the garden with a heavenly perfume. One called 'Evening Fragrance' is well worth seeking out. Newer hybrids, such as the 'Nicki' and 'Domino' series, stay open all day and make a fantastic display but are not noticeably fragrant. Hybrids come in white, crimson, red, pale and deep pink and a lovely lime-green colour. Get the best of both worlds by planting hybrids for a bright daytime display, but scatter some of the perfumed type around the garden.

DM: This is most attractive grown in quantity in the shady spots of a large garden, where it provides late-season bloom.

MO: One of the most appealing annuals for shade, it lends itself to rustic designs and settings. A large relative, *Nicotiana sylvestris*, is available but rarely seen. It never fails to cause comments, with its imposing stature and mops of intensely fragrant white flowers.

LS: My favourites. I love the fragrance on those close summer nights.

RV: May tolerate some shade and is good in sunny locations. The selection 'Lime Green' could become addictive in the Edmonton area.

CJ: This does best in full sun around Vancouver; an excellent bedding plant.

Viola wittrockiana

(pansy)

Pansies have received a lot of attention from plant breeders in recent years, and the resulting explosion of new colours and combinations is mind-boggling. It seems as if almost any colour between white and nearly black is available. Many of the new varieties also hold up quite well in the humid heat of summer. Keep them well watered during hot spells.

DM: Pansies will add lasting colour and bounce to any garden as long as the old flower heads are routinely removed. They bloom almost until snowfall, and some of the plants will overwinter to bring early spring flowers. They also tolerate dreary cold spells that hamper gardening efforts in May and June.

65

MO: Every year brings new combinations of colours. Their cold tolerance allows us to plant them in mid-April, and they bloom from the end of May until frost. Replant each year for compact and vigorous growth.

RV: Suitable for shady borders.

CJ: What are sold on the West Coast as "winter pansies" appear in garden centres here in the fall and will bloom on and off all winter, depending on the weather we get. Spring pansies, which are more heat-tolerant than winter pansies, are sold with primroses beginning about March. If the summer is not too hot, they will bloom until the fall. Otherwise, they fade out around July.

Spring Bulbs

Chionodoxa spp

(glory-of-the-snow)

This is one of the first of the spring-flowering bulbs. The commonest species is *Chionodoxa luciliae*, which has blue flowers. The form 'Pink Giant' is often available and the white one rarely. Plant 3 inches deep in well-drained soil in a situation where they can be left to grow and increase. Lift and divide only when they become overcrowded.

DM: For light to moderate shade, this is a good performer, even self-seeding.

MO: It is perfect for naturalizing in the shade. Plant in association with a nice ground cover such as small hostas or sweet woodruff to avoid disturbing the bulbs while working the ground.

LS: One of the best for naturalizing under deep-rooted trees.

RV: A welcome addition to the spring garden, *Chionodoxa luciliae gigantea* persists here indefinitely without division.

CJ: This is a delightful and accommodating little plant, lovely under rhododendrons and other shrubs.

Crocus tomasinianus

(Tomasin's crocus)

More refined than the large-flowered crocus, this species has blooms of pale lavender with a white throat. It seeds freely, and many forms and variations exist. There are several named selections, among the best of which are 'Barr's Purple,' a rich lilac-purple; the very free-flowering 'Ruby Giant,' with deep violet-purple flowers; and the reddish purple 'Whitewell Purple.'

DM: This species does well in St. John's. Performance is good, even in a north-facing location.

MO: Not tried.

LS: Always popular and widely used in southwestern Ontario.

RV: Winter-killed without flowering. On the other hand, the *Crocus chrysanthus* cultivars 'E.A. Bowles' and 'Zwanenburg Bronze' have persisted (but not flourished) for some 10 years.

CJ: Tomasin's crocus is an excellent crocus for naturalizing in the garden. It spreads well and seeds itself.

Crocus vernus

(spring crocus)

This is the wild crocus of the Alps and the Pyrenees, where it is seen in large drifts of colour ranging from white to a deep purple. It flowers at 3 inches tall, and

the foliage dies down quickly, making it ideal for planting in the lawn or for growing in drifts under shrubs or between perennials. Many named varieties have been introduced, of which 'Jeanne d'Arc' is one of the oldest and best known.

DM: Place these easy bulbs around the base of a small tree or in medium shade, and enjoy the variety of spring colour.

MO: Not tried.

LS: This crocus is also popular and widely used.

RV: The variety *Crocus vernus neapolitanus* persisted and flowered extremely well for several years.

CJ: Spring crocus is more often planted than Tomasin's crocus, and their blooming signals the beginning of spring around Vancouver. They spread gradually and seem to have no faults.

Eranthis hyemalis

(winter aconite)

Bright yellow buttercuplike blooms sit on a ruff of lacy green foliage atop short stems. It usually flowers with the snow-drops, and once established in a moist, woodsy soil, it will seed itself around quite happily. I know some fortunate gardeners who consider this delightful harbinger of spring to be almost a weed, but getting it started can be difficult. The pea-sized tubers are usually badly dried out when purchased and need soaking in warm water for 24 hours before planting. Cover with an inch of loose, friable soil, and water the area well after planting.

DM: This species has been grown here for many years and will spread nicely if dusted annually with bone meal. Flowering as soon as the snow melts, it is suited to planting where there will be considerable overhead shade later in the season.

MO: Undemanding and inexpensive, *Eranthis hyemalis* should be planted by the hundreds. Try them beneath a creeping but nonaggressive ground cover such as *Lysimachia nummularia*.

LS: Always a welcome sight in early spring. Needs very good drainage. Mulch 67

well until it becomes established.

RV: Not hardy on the prairies.

CJ: Winter aconite performs inconsistently in local gardens. For some gardeners, it seeds itself and spreads, but for others, it vanishes. It seems to do best in partial shade and rich, organic soil that does not dry out.

Galanthus nivalis

(snowdrop)

Like winter aconites, snowdrops are easy to grow if you can get them established. Once again, the problem is the dried-out state of most of the bulbs that are sold. Snowdrops are less tolerant of drying out than most bulbs. Ideally, they should be planted "in the green," which means soon after flowering, when the foliage is still green. Snowdrops like moisture and will even do well in quite heavy clay soils. Plant 2 to 3 inches deep, and when planting dried-out bulbs in the fall, water thoroughly after planting.

DM: In old Newfoundland gardens, several plantings have survived for decades. Snowdrops enjoy medium to deep shade under maples, cherries and birches.

MO: Not easy to establish. Only one-third of the first planting I tried came up. They need to be planted as soon as the bulbs become available in order for them to develop good roots before freeze-up. Once established, they come back faithfully each year.

LS: Easy to grow. The double form is a charmer.

RV: *Galanthus nivalis* is not grown in Edmonton. *G. elwesii*, the giant snowdrop, intermittently flowered well over a period of eight years before disappearing.

CJ: Immensely popular, snowdrops naturalize in some gardens, but their numbers are reduced by narcissus bulb fly in other areas.

Muscari armeniacum

(grape hyacinth)

Few bulbs are easier to grow. Grape hyacinths thrive in a wide range of soils and in sun or light shade; if these plants are left in one place, they are guaranteed to multiply rapidly. The 6-to-8-inch flower spikes are lovely when they are massed under spring-flowering shrubs or along a path. They can be lifted and replanted in August when they become overcrowded. They can also be propagated by seed in autumn. The named selections offered for sale include the very free-flowering 'Blue Spike,' with soft blue double flowers, and the pale blue, sweetly scented 'Cantab.'

DM: This species is easy, spreads nicely and persists for many years in light to medium shade and rich ground.

MO: Muscari have not been tried in our shade garden.

LS: A showing of grape hyacinth is another welcome sight come spring. Relatively easy to establish.

RV: An attractive self-seeding bulb and most satisfactory in the prairies. Named cultivars are just as reliable.

CJ: Easy and popular, grape hyacinths combine well with leopard's bane for a cheerful spring picture. They are also nice for small posies.

Narcissus spp and hybrids

(daffodil)

The golden beauty of the daffodil needs no introduction. Daffodils and spring go hand in hand, whether it is a potful to brighten a balcony or the massed planting of a grassy slope or woodland floor. Do look for and try some of the more unusual ones that are becoming increasingly available. There is a daffodil to suit your every need, from the 3-inch-tall *Narcissus minimus*, with tiny flowers to match, to the large, showy 2-foot-tall hybrids, with blooms measuring 5½ inches across. Plant in well-drained soil as soon as bulbs are available in the fall, especially in cold areas. If the weather is dry, water the planting well. Daffodils must make roots in the fall and need several weeks to do this before freeze-up.

DM: In general, narcissi are easy to cultivate, and they flourish in our moist, cool climate. Dig up and divide old clumps to keep them flowering.

MO: A wide choice is available, most of which will do well in the shade garden.

The hybrids of *Narcissus triandrus* need more sun and should be avoided. Daffodil leaves must be allowed to ripen and die down naturally, but if planted among perennials such as hostas, they are hidden during this ugly stage. Steady moisture must be available, because the late-blooming double varieties may suffer from dried-up buds that fail to open if hot weather and drying winds occur at flowering time.

LS: A great variety is available, extending far beyond the typical 'King Alfred.'

RV: Many cultivars do well for a few seasons and then disappear. Our season in Edmonton is normally too short to allow for enlargement of bulbs. It is therefore futile to lift and divide bulbs and best to simply add a few new bulbs each fall in order to maintain a flowering population. *Narcissus poeticus* has been one of the most satisfactory in this area.

CJ: As is true in most of the world, daffodils and tulips are the most popular spring-flowering bulbs. In some parts of our area, daffodils naturalize, yet in some gardens (regrettably, mine is one of them), they are destroyed by narcissus bulb fly in a matter of seasons. Chemical control of this pest is expensive and certainly not environmentally friendly. The mechanical means that I have tried, such as moving the bulbs to a screened frame once they have finished blooming, are effective but a nuisance. In this area, it is best to see what the pest situation is like in the garden before planting too many.

Scilla sibirica

(Siberian squill)

This is one of the most popular of the early spring-flowering bulbs. A well-established patch of Siberian squill can be a stunning sight. They are about 8 inches tall with up to six brilliant blue flowers on each stem, and they often produce several stems from each bulb. The deep, rich blue 'Spring Beauty' is the best-known selection. Plant about 4 inches deep. They will do well in any reasonable garden soil.

DM: This bulb is perfectly hardy here,

spreading out in a lightly shaded site. The bright blue spikes are very showy. Also grown here is the somewhat more subtle *Scilla tubergeniana*.

MO: They perform very well and are one of the few bulbs that can withstand dry shade.

LS: A good one to naturalize under trees, especially deep-rooted ones.

RV: Very satisfactory.

CJ: Delightful dwarf plants with bright blue flowers to liven up even the dullest corner in early spring. Easy to obtain and to grow.

Trillium spp

(wake robin, trillium)

Chosen as the floral emblem of Ontario, the trillium carpets our woodlands in white every spring. The flowers last about a month, fading to pale pink before they wither and turn brown. Easy to grow in the garden, trilliums do well in a moist but well-drained soil rich in organic matter. Sandy loams with lots of leaf mould are good, as is any decent well-drained garden soil with a good layer of compost worked into the top 8 inches.

DM: Trilliums are difficult to maintain in St. John's. Perhaps the season or the soil is too cold, too wet or too acidic, for these plants just linger pitifully and never put on a strong display.

MO: A pocket of rich, humusy soil sheltered from the wind will be to their liking, and a ground cover of gaultheria or wild ginger will clothe their leggy stems. *Trillium grandiflorum* and *T. erectum* are the most readily available. If you find the double form *T. grandiflorum* 'Flore Pleno' in some specialist nursery, it is easy to grow and one to treasure. *T. undulatum* needs more acidic conditions and is difficult to maintain in the garden.

LS: Give them lots of humus and afternoon shade, and they are not difficult to establish in the garden.

RV: Native *Trillium grandiflorum* does well in a woodsy soil, flowering in May. Suited to shady wild meadow gardens.

CJ: Trilliums are protected here and can only be acquired at garden-club or botanical-garden sales when they have been rescued from wooded areas faced with bulldozers. They are easy to grow from seed but take seven years to bloom, which accounts for their special status.

Ferns

Adiantum pedatum

(maidenhair fern)

Found growing wild from Nova Scotia to Minnesota, this is one of the daintiest of our northeastern ferns. If planted in a rich, well-drained, humusy soil, it will remain attractive from spring to fall. Branching rhizomes creep just below the soil surface, but it spreads slowly and will not become a problem.

DM: This is not a plant for the novice gardener in eastern Newfoundland. Grow in a protected site where the relative humidity remains high and fragile fronds are not pulverized by our drying, driving westerly wind. Give morning sun or dappled shade.

MO: One of our prettiest native ferns. Makes a good ground cover underplanted with spring-flowering bulbs that can ripen their foliage before the wiry black stems and fanlike leaves develop. If you have a small nook where something daintier is

71

needed, *Adiantum pedatum aleuticum* could prove to be the perfect choice.

LS: This is the most delicate fern, but you must have a moist, shaded location and a soil rich in humus.

RV: Maidenhair is only borderline hardy and short-lived in Edmonton.

CJ: A native fern loved by all who know it, maidenhair is a good introduction for gardeners who have not yet discovered ferns. It is virtually foolproof when grown in shade and tolerates surprisingly dry soil.

Athyrium nipponicum pictum

(Japanese painted fern)

This fern (often listed as *A. goeringianum pictum* in catalogues) is prized for its delicately coloured new fronds, which are a soft metallic grey suffused with reddish or bluish undertones. A silver central stripe looks rather as if it has been deliberately painted onto the mature fronds, hence the common name. It prefers a shady location in humus-rich loam; plants in light shade develop the best colour.

DM: We do not grow this one in eastern Newfoundland.

MO: The only variegated fern that is

readily available in the trade. It goes through every winter and comes back each spring with even bigger clumps of silvery foliage and wine-red stems. If it is grown in full sun, the fronds will be stunted and greyish, showing the need for shade. Peaty soils that stay moist will please it.

LS: I am not that familiar with this one.

RV: Not grown and probably not hardy.

CJ: This cultivar won't survive severe winters, like the one of 1990-91. However, like other unusual ferns, it is becoming more readily available.

Dryopteris filix-mas

(male fern)

A stately native fern commonly found both here and in Europe, *Dryopteris filix-mas* looks lovely with tall foxgloves and deserves a place in any shade garden. Although it will tolerate dry shade when once established, it will be happier in deep, humusy, constantly damp soil with small stones and rocks mixed through it. The smaller crested shield fern (*D. cristata*) and leatherwood fern (*D. marginalis*) are also good in similar conditions.

DM: A native plant suited to a woodland

72

garden, it does best in organic soil with plenty of leaf mould.

MO: Reaching a height of 3 feet when well grown, this fern should be used more frequently as an accent plant. The clumps spread slowly, forming a vase-shaped cluster of fronds that are almost evergreen and last well into the autumn. It has great adaptability and is a good one to try if your previous attempts to grow ferns have been unsuccessful.

LS: I think *Dryopteris marginalis* is a bolder, more interesting species.

RV: An occasional woodland native in Alberta but not well adapted to gardens. At the botanic garden, we found *Dryopteris marginalis* to be quite satisfactory.

CJ: Male fern does well even in heavy shade, and it likes moist soil.

Matteuccia struthiopteris

(ostrich fern)

Found in marshy areas and along streams and ditches, this fern seems to grow in any shady spot with good moist soil. Garden plants will usually be around 2 to 3 feet tall, but it can reach 4 feet in optimum conditions. Provide plenty of water to keep it looking its best into late summer. The black fertile fronds are much coveted by flower arrangers.

DM: Rich but well-drained soil and filtered sun will allow this species to create a lush foliage effect.

MO: One of the easiest ferns to accommodate and a perfect ground cover. Providing the soil is moist, it will grow in sun or shade. Be warned: If you pick fiddleheads from your ornamental planting, limit picking to two per plant to ensure that each specimen continues to thrive.

LS: If you have a moist acre or two with some shade, fill it with fiddleheads and assure yourself of an annual supply of this great delicacy. A really bold fern for any moist, shaded area.

RV: By far the most common fern grown in this region, in spite of its ugly black fertile fronds and a strong tendency for its underground stolons to invade lawns.

CJ: A handsome plant that adds drama to the garden. It spreads but can easily be contained by a bottomless wooden box sunk to soil level.

Climbers

Aristolochia durior

(Dutchman's pipe)

Dutchman's pipe has been used for screening or shading front porches since it was introduced to Europe by John Bartram in 1783. The vigorous climbing, twining vines grow from 20 to 30 feet, making it an ideal plant for this use. It will happily twine itself over any porch, trellis, arbour or pergola in a single season. The strange flowers are unusual in both shape and colour, looking rather like a yellow-green and brownish purple meerschaum pipe. Growing in full sun or partial shade, its value is in the shade it can provide on a sunny lot.

DM: Local experience is limited.

MO: The rough texture of the big heart-shaped leaves makes this a very attractive climber. It will grow in most soils but is slow to become established. Once it takes

73

ued trees and shrubs, but I have seen it pruned to form a delightful entrance tunnel to a city garden. It is best planted in poor soil for controllable growth.

DM: This climber grows remarkably well in considerable shade.

MO: Bittersweet is among the easiest of climbers to care for and grow. Besides the orange seed capsules that are used for winter decoration, the foliage turns a pale yellow in autumn. If you plant this, remember that the sexes are on different plants and you should have one male plant for every six to eight females.

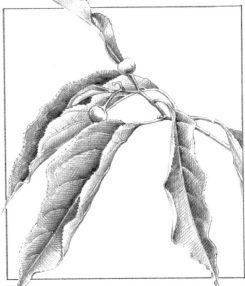

LS: It is always nice to be able to pick a few clusters of the dried orange-coloured fruits in the fall to use for winter bouquets.

RV: This is well established at the Devonian Botanic Garden in a sandy soil.

CJ: This vine is not as successful on the West Coast as it is farther east.

Lonicera brownii 'Dropmore Scarlet'

(climbing honeysuckle)

Raised by F.L. Skinner in his nursery at Dropmore, Manitoba, 'Dropmore Scarlet' is the hardiest of the vine honeysuckles. The 2-inch-long, trumpet-shaped flowers are scarlet outside with orange interiors and are produced from midsum-

hold, however, it grows rapidly. It is a dense covering climber that deserves to be planted more often.

LS: If you want a mass of foliage to provide privacy for a porch or a shaded area, this is the plant to use.

RV: Dutchman's pipe is well established on a north-facing garage wall.

CJ: Although not readily available for sale, there is an excellent example of this striking vine in the arbour walk at the UBC Botanical Gardens.

Celastrus scandens

(bittersweet)

A woody twining vine valued more for its bright orange-red seed capsules than for its small greenish yellow flowers, *Celastrus scandens* can be found growing wild over much of eastern North America in sandy or rocky woods, in swampy thickets, on roadsides and slopes and along fencerows. It thrives in both moist and dry situations and is a useful vine in the home garden for scrambling over fences and old trees or covering unsightly rock piles. If carelessly placed, it is quite capable of smothering or strangling valmer until frost. It takes a year or two for the deciduous, woody-stemmed climber to become established, but then it grows quite fast. Some nurseries list it as 'Scarlet Trumpet' honeysuckle.

DM: This climber provides continuous bloom throughout the season; a few trumpets have been known to persist into December. It is quick to establish itself and is ideal for concealing a trellised wall. Give direct sunlight for half a day to produce ample flowers.

MO: If you are looking for a climber with a prolonged blooming period, this one might be the answer. It blooms from June until first frost, and the bright orange flowers are very striking. Growth is quite stiff, and it does best against a trellis or open-weave fence.

LS: I know one plant that lived for over 15 years growing in a large planter on an east-facing 18th-floor balcony in downtown Toronto. It flowered profusely and continuously every summer.

RV: 'Dropmore Scarlet' is reasonably hardy but appears to be susceptible to a virus that results in chlorosis and decline.

CJ: There are several good climbing honeysuckles available here, including *Lonicera japonica aureoreticulata*, *L. j. halliana*, *L. j. purpurea* and *L. periclymenum*

var. *belgica* and *serotina*. All are valued for their fragrance and ease of care.

Parthenocissus quinquefolia

(Virginia creeper)

Often seen covering the walls of universities and older homes, this attractive deciduous vine can almost cement itself to walls. New growth is a bronzy red, turning to a deep, lustrous green in summer and then to a purplish or crimson red in fall. The bluish black berries add interest after the leaves have fallen. Tolerant of almost any kind of soil and polluted city conditions, this vine will grow in full sun or full shade. The closely related Boston ivy (*Parthenocissus tricuspidata*) is not as hardy but is slightly more attractive.

DM: The only special note is to protect against wild winds and winter ice buildup.

MO: The glossy compound leaves smother not only walls and buildings but also lawns and other plants. It has a rampageous habit, but the rich scarlet leaves in the fall help us to forget the way it runs.

LS: It is pretty hard to beat the bright, glossy, dark green leaves of this vine.

RV: Grows best in sheltered locations.

CJ: The West Coast forests are not particularly noted for vivid fall colour, so Virginia creeper always impresses local gardeners. It is easy to grow and can be used as a ground cover as well as a vine.

Shrubs

Amelanchier spp

(Juneberry, saskatoon)

Thriving in ordinary garden soil or in wetter areas along the margins of streams and lakes, saskatoons can be grown as understorey shrubs in light shade or planted in sun and pruned into small trees to provide dappled shade. The milky white, cherrylike blossoms open before the leaves unfurl to give an enchanting, if fleeting, display. Good for encouraging birds into the garden, the fruit can be both attractive and delicious but is usually stripped off by our feathered friends as it ripens.

DM: There are several native species and hybrids of these shrubs, known in Newfoundland as chuckley pears. Naturally found at the woods' edge, these shrubs will flower and fruit well in light shade or partial sun. Good forms with

large or extra petals are easy to find locally. My favourite, *Amelanchier bartramiana*, is a small-statured plant with large rounded flowers, ruby-coloured spring foliage and abundant sugary fruit.

MO: A short blooming period makes this a fleeting beauty, but it can be valuable in a shady situation. Not in the least demanding, it sometimes suckers freely to form a thicket.

LS: Always a welcome note for the arrival of spring, particularly when one has a chance to drive out in the southern Ontario countryside and see their white flowers against the otherwise grey woods.

RV: *Amelanchier alnifolia* is the hardy species and is, in fact, a common native plant at the botanic garden. Those selections with superior fruit, such as 'Smoky' and 'Pembina,' are more often grown than plants from the wild. The only problem with saskatoons is a smut disease that in some years blackens the leaves, making them hang on all winter, and a tendency to moderate root suckering.

CJ: Members of this genus are not widely grown on the West Coast, but robins enjoy their berries, and with the current increasing interest in gardening for wildlife, they may become more popular. They seem to do best here in full sun.

Cornus alba

(Tatarian dogwood)

This Asian counterpart of our native dogwood is an invaluable member of the shade garden. It is one of the few plants whose variegated forms will keep their bright colours in shade – the majority of variegated plants turn green unless in bright sunlight. The variety *Cornus alba argenteo-marginata* (usually sold as *C. a. elegantissima*) has leaves splashed in white, *C. a. gouchaultii* has leaves mottled with yellow and pink, and *C. a. spaethii* has leaves edged with yellow. They also have reddish winter twigs, although they are admittedly not as bright as those of the native dogwood.

DM: For decorative red twigs, you can't

beat the native red osier dogwood (see *Cornus sericea*).

MO: Among the easiest of shrubs for shade. *Cornus alba argenteo-marginata*, with its silver variegated leaves, and *C. a. spaethii*, with golden variegated leaves, are widely used in foundation plantings to give foliage interest during the summer.

LS: The species itself is of no special note, but several varieties are. *Cornus alba sibirica* is good for winter interest with its colourful red twigs, and *C. a. argenteo-marginata* is a most effective shrub for colour contrast in light to medium shade. Red twigs are also attractive.

RV: Selections of *Cornus alba* often perform well but are subject to winter dieback following test winters. The variety *C. a. sibirica* has the most attractive coral-red bark. Several foliage variants are popular, the best being *C. a. argenteo-marginata* with its blotched leaves edged with white. For best results, provide them all with adequate moisture and some shelter, as well as shade.

CJ: The most popular and readily available Tatarian dogwood in southern British Columbia is the variegated *Cornus alba*

argenteo-marginata. It is a large shrub, so it should be pruned regularly if grown in the home garden.

Cornus sericea

(red osier dogwood)

This native plant thrives naturally in wet areas, but it will grow quite happily in drier soils. The intensity of stem colour varies from plant to plant, so be selective and look for the brightest forms when shopping for this one. Cutting the stems back almost to ground level every three or four years will ensure that new growth has the best colour. For yellow twigs that appear to glow in the late-afternoon sun, use the variety *Cornus sericea flaviramea*. Plant where the winter effect can be seen and enjoyed from indoors.

DM: Red osier dogwood is a native plant that flourishes in open areas alongside streams and river systems, where there is a source of moving water – somewhat fresher and more nutrient-rich than stagnant boggy ground. In landscape plantings, these shrubs are used in drier sites; the growth is more restrained but very ornamental. In areas where winters are long, it is important to include shrubs 77 like these with a year-round landscape effect. Tolerates a north or east wall.

MO: The coloured twigs of *Cornus sericea flaviramea* can make a subtle portrait during the fall and winter months, especially when used with a form of *C. alba* with red twigs. Cut back the older stems each spring for brightly coloured new growth.

LS: Noted for its coloured twigs – red in the species, yellow in the selection *C. s. flaviramea.*

RV: Native to the prairies, this is one of the best medium-sized shrubs for the off-season. Autumn foliage turns a prominent wine-red, and in the winter, the stems show up bright red against the snow. The yellow-twigged form, *C. s. flaviramea*, is equally tough. Old scurfy branches should be ruthlessly removed in order to encourage new growth with fresh, colourful bark.

CJ: *Cornus sericea* is represented most often by the variety *flaviramea*, which is not as readily available as the forms of *C. alba*. Both are used extensively in commercial landscaping projects, most often in full sun.

Daphne mezereum

(February daphne)

One of the hardiest of the daphnes, this small, attractive plant is also one of the first spring shrubs to bloom. Clusters of purple-pink, intensely fragrant flowers open before the foliage appears, quite often as the last of the snow melts, to be followed by scarlet berries. Branches cut from a mature bush to force into bloom indoors will scent the entire house. Grow in a loose, sandy soil with perfect drainage, but supply enough water to keep the soil relatively cool and moist. Keep an eye open for seedlings as you weed. A white form with creamy white flowers and yellow berries is sometimes available. 'Paul's White' and 'Bowles' White' are two selections with pure white flowers.

DM: Daphne flowers are fragrant and very early; in Newfoundland, that means late April or early May. This shrub grows well here with only a little direct sunlight,

and it self-seeds too. Move only when young, because older shrubs are almost impossible to transplant.

MO: *Daphne mezereum* bears spring flowers all along the stem, which are followed by bright red but toxic berries. Hardy in Montreal but has a reputation for being temperamental; branches occasionally die back without apparent cause.

LS: The fragrance and colour on bleak early-spring days are always welcome.

RV: This is borderline hardy, so it is recommended only for exceptionally sheltered sites near buildings and on the north side for snow cover.

CJ: On the West Coast, the nursery-people joke that it is the only shrub in the nursery to be potted into a smaller pot each year! In the garden, its performance is inconsistent. In some gardens, it fails to thrive; in others, it succeeds and even seeds itself.

Hydrangea arborescens 'Annabelle'

(Annabelle hydrangea)

This variety was introduced because it flowers earlier than the closely related

Hydrangea arborescens grandiflora, although both will do well in light shade. It grows more like a herbaceous perennial in most parts of Canada, being winter-killed almost to ground level each winter and growing back rapidly in the spring. By late June, it is covered with globes of white flowers. The flowers go from white to green to brown as they age and can be cut at any of these stages and dried for winter bouquets.

DM: The cultivar with snowball flower clusters that has been grown here over many years is *Hydrangea arborescens grandiflora*. It will tolerate partial shade. The more recent compact selection 'Annabelle' is little known in our area.

MO: The ubiquitous presence of *Hydrangea arborescens* 'Annabelle' in shade gardens all around Montreal proves it to be a perfect choice for an early-summer-blooming shrub in shade. *H. quercifolia* is not completely hardy in this area, but it is worth trying in sheltered gardens for its shapely and corrugated foliage, which takes on striking plum tints in autumn.

LS: I still remember the first time I was shown a plant in full flower in the nursery at Hamilton's Royal Botanical Gardens. We featured a photograph of it in *Ornamental Shrubs for Canada*, and it has since become widely grown and used in Canada. Excellent for drying for winter bouquets.

RV: This takes a few years to become established, but the patient gardener will be well rewarded. Eye-catching white ball flower heads develop by late summer, when they are most appreciated. Cut the tops back as you would a herbaceous perennial.

CJ: Although not widely grown, 'Annabelle' is an easy and adaptable shrub that blooms reliably on the West Coast.

Rhododendron spp and hybrids

(rhododendron and azalea)

In native habitats where conditions are right, rhododendrons grow like weeds. They can cover acres of ground with an impenetrable mass of bushes officially called a rhododendron hell. I struggled to change natural conditions to suit them in Ottawa, and my pride and joy was a few puny bushes any Vancouver gardener would have thrown out. Given an acidic, woodsy soil, a mild climate and summer shade, these aristocrats of the shade garden are easy to grow; without such conditions, they will not thrive.

DM: There are many rhododendrons to choose from, provided that the soil is amended to a mix of 50 percent peat. If drainage is a problem, incorporate some coarse sand as well. The dwarf types require at least partial sun to maintain tight growth and abundant bloom. Easy to grow are 'Ramapo,' 'Grand Pré,' *Rhododendron impeditum*, *R. fastigiatum*, *R. ferrugineum*, *R. tapetiforme* and *R. yakusimanum*. For moderate shade, try *R. carolinianum* or *R. dauricum*. Somewhat taller selections for filtered light or the edge of the woods are old standards such as *R. roseum elegans*, *R. catawbiense album* and 'P.J.M.' Newer ones are 'Besse Howells,' 'Vernus' and 'Wyandanch.' Hardy, deciduous species for a partly shaded garden are *R. camtschaticum*, *R. vaseyi*,

79

R. schlippenbachii and our native pink or white *R. canadense*.

MO: These are plants for the keen gardener around Montreal. The only evergreen one I consider worthwhile and not risky to plant is 'P.J.M.' With deciduous types, the choice is wider, and I would recommend *Rhododendron mucronulatum* and especially the cultivar 'Cornell Pink.' The 'Light' series of azaleas, such as 'Northern Lights,' developed by the University of Minnesota, are also proving reliable in light shade.

LS: Rhododendrons are a challenge in zones 5 and 6, particularly in areas that do not have light, sandy, naturally acidic soil. A real challenge but well worth the effort if you succeed in establishing the needed conditions. It is always a pleasure to visit coastal British Columbia and see them growing so "naturally."

RV: With the possible exception of the deciduous *Rhododendron canadense*, with its rather inconspicuous rose-purple flowers, and the much-praised selection 'P.J.M.,' "rhodies" have not been worth the garden space or trouble on the prairies.

CJ: Evergreen rhododendrons and azaleas reign in coastal British Columbia gardens. From showy hybrids, with huge, breathtaking trusses, to exquisite dwarf species, the selection boggles the mind and is increasing every year. Virtually the only cultural problem they face on the coast is leaf notching by root weevils. Deciduous azaleas are also very popular here. There are some gardens in Vancouver that you need sunglasses to behold in May, so vivid are the contrasting yellows, scarlets, oranges and hot pinks.

Ribes spp

(flowering currant)

In much of Canada, it is the yellow-flowered golden currant (*Ribes aureum*) and clove currant (*R. odoratum*) that are prized for their fragrant spring blooms. In the milder climate of the West Coast, named forms of the native scarlet currant (*R. sanguineum*) are more common. The alpine currant (*R. alpinum*) is often used for hedges, especially in the Montreal area, and seems equally at home in sun or shade. All do well in any reasonably good soil.

DM: Most currants do well in St. John's and are tolerant of a wide range of condi-

tions. To encourage blooms, give flowering currants sun for half the day.

MO: *Ribes odoratum* and *R. alpinum* have been tried in the shade garden, but we are gradually getting rid of them to leave space for choicer candidates. Nevertheless, *R. alpinum* is a valuable hedge plant for shady conditions. *R. odoratum*'s susceptibility to black spot has proved detrimental in shade or other situations where air circulation is poor. In bad years, it is almost naked by the end of August.

LS: Alpine currant is definitely the best deciduous shrub for use as a hedge in shaded areas and is also good for massing. Grows well in full sun also. Flowering currant is a truly old-fashioned shrub; I can remember one in my grandparents' garden. The red fall colour is spectacular.

RV: *Ribes aureum*, the golden-flowered currant, is a reliable plant for the shade garden. Be prepared to prune it back annually to keep it within bounds. Unfortunately, the red-flowered *R. sanguineum* is not hardy on the prairies.

CJ: A native shrub, flowering currant is popular with many gardeners and is easy to grow. Its blooms attract hummingbirds and remind bird watchers to put out their hummingbird feeders.

Symphoricarpos spp

(snowberry)

Growing from 3 to 6 feet tall, the snowberry is tolerant of almost any soil, including clay. The flowers are small and pale pink and are not at all attention-grabbers, but I find them attractive. In the fall and early winter, the snowberry comes into its own with clusters of large white berries, adding interest to the landscape. In regions where the snow comes early, use one of the pink-fruited forms, such as 'Mother of Pearl,' which show up better against the snow. Watch for seedlings growing in the middle of other shrubs. Birds must spread the seed in winter, because this is the worst shrub I know of for germinating in awkward locations.

DM: *Symphoricarpos albus* is very tough and very easy. Large old plants can make good fruiting specimens in open sites and perform well when trimmed as a hedgerow in deep shade. This shrub produces a dramatic effect of showy "pearls" after the foliage drops, even late in November.

MO: This is planted extensively in the Montreal area and is very good for naturalized plantings. The hybrid 'Hancock,' introduced by the late Les Hancock of Mississauga, Ontario, is currently marketed and widely planted here but suffers regular winterkill on some branches.

LS: I never used to get excited by these until I started seeing mass plantings in parking lots. The white fruit really stands out through fall and winter.

RV: *Symphoricarpos albus* is a low-growing native species appreciated for its ornamental snow-white berries. Buckbrush (*S. occidentalis*) is a taller and more vigorous (read "weedy") plant, the berries having an off-white, sallow appearance.

CJ: Although this is a common native plant, it is not widely grown in home gardens. It may become more popular with gardeners who are trying to attract and feed birds through the winter.

Taxus spp

(yew)

Three species of yew are grown as ornamentals in Canada. The English yew (*Taxus baccata*) is hardy only on the West

Coast, but the Japanese yew (*T. cuspidata*) is much hardier and can be tried in sheltered locations on the prairies. The hybrid between these two, *T. media*, is almost as hardy as the Japanese yew. There are many named forms of this hybrid in shapes ranging from spreading to columnar. All need fertile soil and sufficient moisture but excellent drainage. Yews do badly and may possibly die if planted in poorly drained sites.

DM: Several cultivars of *Taxus media* are reliably hardy in St. John's. Excellent specimens result if given half sun. Too much overhead shade results in thin plants, due to lack of light and moisture. Try partial shade for a portion of the day or side light at the edge of a woodland.

MO: Frequently used for hedges and foundation plantings, they provide a dark background that sets off plants with lighter foliage. Warm spells in March, while the ground is still frozen, can cause considerable browning of the needles. To avoid this problem, water copiously in the fall and plant where they will not be subjected to winter sun.

LS: One cannot say enough about this group of evergreens. The yews form the backbone of any foundation planting on the east or north side of a building. Most people do not realize they can do equally well in sunny areas. The smaller needles and the "tufted" texture make *T. nigra* stand out. Slow-growing, so it won't get out of bounds; this is my favourite.

RV: For prairie gardeners with shelter, shade and well-drained soil who would like at least one representative from milder climes, the yew will do very well. The hardiest but least desirable as a garden ornamental is the low-growing Canadian yew (*Taxus canadensis*). With the cooler weather of autumn, this species turns an indescribable off-colour. Nice, with its rich, glossy foliage (but needing the comfort of a nearby wall), is the Japanese yew (*T. cuspidata*). It may be either upright or of spreading habit.

CJ: The Rolls-Royce of hedging materials, yew is not as widely planted as cedar because of the cost, especially for larger plants. If you have the budget and the patience, it makes a magnificent hedge and a classic backdrop for perennial or mixed borders. *Taxus media hicksii* is the variety most often grown. The spreading English yew (*T. baccata repandens*) is a handsome shrub for shade and should be grown more often.

Viburnum spp

(viburnum)

A large group of shrubs with an endless variety of uses, viburnums are among my favourites. Some are valued solely for their flowers, which may be in globes or flat clusters and can be fragrant; others also have attractive fruit to provide winter colour and bring birds into the garden; and many have good fall colour. Most are tolerant of shade or sun, and they are a useful group for growing as understorey shrubs in shade or for providing shade under which to grow less heat-tolerant plants.

DM: There are several native species well worth having in your garden. They tolerate a moderate amount of shade, such

as at a woods' edge, and enjoy a damp site. My favourite is the 6-foot withe-rod (*Viburnum cassinoides*), with its shiny, leathery leaves and showy racemes of creamy flowers. These are followed by berries gradually ripening from green to red to blue-black, producing multicoloured fruit clusters. Fall foliage is a burgundy-wine shade, and winter twigs have decorative buds. The plant holds a tight, even shape without any pruning. A smaller (to 3 feet) species, known as mooseberry or lowbush cranberry (*V. edule*), and the larger (to 9 feet) highbush cranberry (*V. trilobum*) bear juicy red fruit and are attractive to birds. Many other viburnums are available at local nurseries, and most are easy and reliable.

MO: Perfectly hardy, undemanding in their cultural requirements and good for attracting birds. The velvety or corrugated leaves of *Viburnum lantana* 'Mohican' and *V. rhytidophylloides* 'Allegheny' give textural contrast and are about the last to lose their leaves in November. *V. trilobum compactum* would make a noteworthy hedge in shade.

LS: I like nannyberry (*Viburnum lentago*). It is hard to beat the glossy foliage, creamy white flowers, brilliant fall colour and blue-black edible fruit. This is a very large shrub or small tree. Two native species, *V. cassinoides* and *V. dentatum*, are useful for naturalizing in wooded areas.

RV: The native American highbush cranberry (*Viburnum trilobum*) and its European counterpart (*V. opulus*) are grown but can become rampant on moist sites. Fall colour depends on the individual plant and the local climate but can be very attractive. With our trend to smaller lots, the variety *V. trilobum compactum* may be a better choice. The famed snowball bush, with large, round, white flower clusters, is a selection of the European bush cranberry (*V. opulus roseum*). Two other satisfactory species are the nannyberry and the wayfaring tree (*V. lantana*), which has multicoloured fruit.

CJ: There are many excellent ornamental shrubs in this genus. The most widely grown is David's viburnum (*Viburnum davidii*), which is used extensively in commercial projects and home gardens. Plants were damaged in the severe winter of 1990-91, but they are generally winterhardy. This shrub does well in shade and dryish soil, making it useful for planting along the north side of a house. Also evergreen and readily available, *V. tinus* appears more susceptible to frost damage than *V. davidii*. Five other viburnums are available in many garden centres. *V. plicatum mariesii* (doublefile viburnum) is very popular, with its tiers of lacy white flowers. *V. bodnantense* 'Dawn' offers fragrant pink flowers in winter, and *V. carlesii* (Korean spice viburnum) and its offspring *V. carlcephalum* and *V. burkwoodii* have superb fragrance. The evergreen leatherleaf viburnum (*V. rhytidophyllum*) is seen in older gardens around Vancouver, but it becomes quite large and also is somewhat difficult to find.

Vinca minor

(lesser periwinkle)

Known as "violet of the sorcerers," periwinkle was once believed to ward off evil

RV: In my home garden in Edmonton, this normally comes through the winter in fine shape and starts to flower, then invariably gets bitten by the sharp frosts of late spring. Possibly a move to deeper shade would dampen this precocity until more equitable temperatures arrive.

CJ: An excellent and readily available foolproof ground cover for shade. Blue- and purple-flowered forms are the most popular, but white is also grown.

Other Shade-Gardening Choices

Perennials

Ajuga reptans (bugleweed)
Anemone sylvestris (wood anemone)
Asarum spp (wild ginger)
Bergenia cordifolia (giant rockfoil)
Cimicifuga racemosa (black snakeroot)
Doronicum cordatum [*caucasicum*]
   (leopard's bane)
Heuchera hybrids (alumroot)
Mertensia virginica (Virginia bluebells)
Omphalodes verna (blue-eyed Mary)
Podophyllum pelatum (Mayapple)
Trollius (globeflower)

Annuals

Lunaria annua (honesty)
Petunia hybrida (petunia)

Bulbs

Camassia (camass)
Colchicum autumnalis
   (false autumn crocus)
Cyclamen coum (Atkins cyclamen)
Hyacinthoides hispanica (Spanish bluebell)
Iris reticulata (netted iris)

Ferns

Osmunda regalis (royal fern)

Climbers

Hydrangea anomala petiolaris
   (climbing hydrangea)

spirits; no witch would dare to enter a door over which a bunch hung. Today, this creeping evergreen is invaluable as a ground cover. It is slow to establish, and you must expect to weed it for several years, but once it forms a dense mat, it is trouble-free. The 30-inch creeping stems root as they spread, and cuttings root easily in a sand and peat mix or simply stuck in a moist, shady bed. There is a variegated form, which is harder to establish.

DM: Dwarf periwinkle is an easy ground cover that forms a dense carpet of evergreen leaves dotted with violet-coloured blooms throughout the season, even late into the fall. It is tolerant of a wide range of sun and shade.

MO: Absolutely hardy, charming plants that are invaluable if you want to create a lush, weed-proof carpet. They cope with every type of soil and need a couple of years to reach their full development.

LS: A good ground cover for shade, where it forms a dense mat. The flowers are colourful.

Shrubs

Hamamelis (witch hazel)
Ilex (holly)
Kerria japonica (Japanese kerria)
Mahonia (Oregon grape)
Paxistima canbyi (Canby's pachistima)
Pieris (pieris)
Sorbaria serbifolia (Ural false spiraea)
Thuja (arborvitae, white cedar)
Tsuga (hemlock)

CLIMATIC ZONE MAPS–CANADA

Lower zone numbers refer to increasingly cold areas, but there are no specific minimum-temperature limits for each zone.

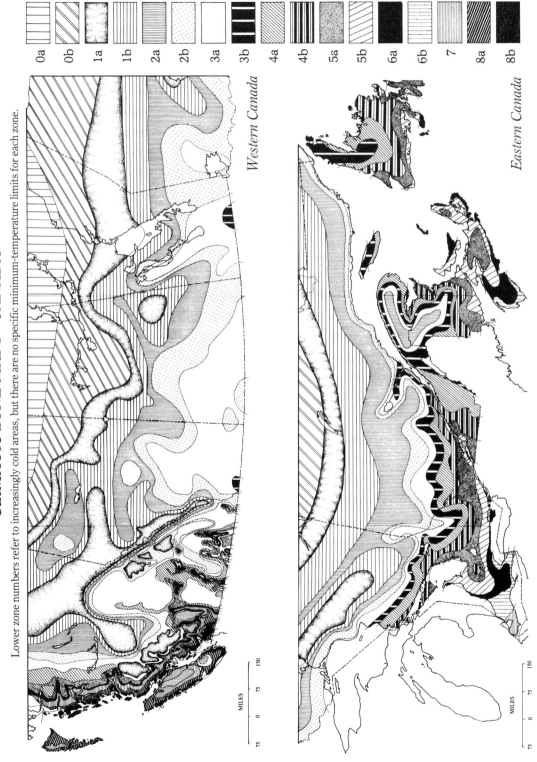

0a	0b	1a	1b	2a	2b	3a
3b	4a	4b	5a	5b	6a	6b
7	8a	8b				

Western Canada

Eastern Canada

MILES
75 0 75 150

MILES
75 0 75 150

86

CLIMATIC ZONE MAP – UNITED STATES

Average minimum temperatures are listed for each zone in Fahrenheit degrees.

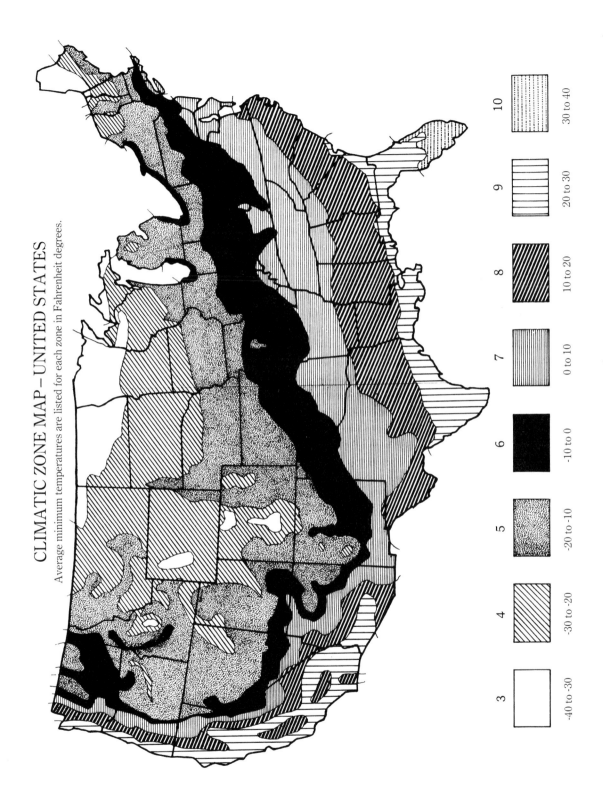

3	4	5	6	7	8	9	10
-40 to -30	-30 to -20	-20 to -10	-10 to 0	0 to 10	10 to 20	20 to 30	30 to 40

Sources

Societies

Alpine Garden Club of B.C.
Box 5161-MPO
Vancouver, British Columbia V6B 4B2

American Primrose Society
9705 S.W. Spring Crest Drive
Portland, Oregon 97225

American Rock Garden Society
Box 67
Millwood, New York 10546-0067

Hardy Plant Society
Bank Cottage, Great Comberton
Nr Pershore
Worcestershire WR10 3DP, England

Ontario Rock Garden Society
Box 146
Shelburne, Ontario L0N 1S0

Books

The Complete Shade Gardener by
George Schenk (Houghton Mifflin Co.;
Boston, 1984).

Gardening in the Shade by Harriet K.
Morse (Timber Press; Oregon, 1982;
revised edition).

The Natural Shade Garden by Ken
Druse (Clarkson N. Potter, Inc.; 1992).

Plants for Shade and Woodland by
Allen Paterson (Fitzhenry &
Whiteside; 1987).

Mail-Order Directory

Mail-order nurseries often stock cultivars that are unavailable locally. While it
is easiest and fastest to order plants from

within one's own country, Canadians wishing to buy from U.S. nurseries can obtain a Permit to Import from The Permit Office, Plant Health Division, Agriculture Canada, Ottawa, Ontario K1A 0C6. One form is necessary for each company from which you order plants.

Imports to the United States must include an invoice showing the quantity and value of the plants, as well as a document from the Department of Agriculture certifying that the plants are disease-free.

Canada

Aimers Seeds
81 Temperance Street
Aurora, Ontario L4G 1R1

Alberta Nurseries & Seeds Ltd.
Box 20
Bowden, Alberta T0M 0K0

Bayport Plant Farm
RR 1
Rose Bay, Nova Scotia B0J 2X0

Brickman's Botanical Gardens
RR 1
Sebringville, Ontario N0K 1K0

The Butchart Gardens Ltd.
Box 4010, Station A
Victoria, British Columbia V8X 3X1

Chiltern Seeds
Bortree Stile, Ulverston
Cumbria LA12 7PB, England

C.A. Cruickshank Inc.
1015 Mt. Pleasant Road
Toronto, Ontario M4P 2M1

Delair Gardens
35120 Delair Road, RR 4
Abbotsford, British Columbia
V2S 4N4

Dominion Seed House
115 Guelph Street
Georgetown, Ontario L7G 4A2

Ferncliff Gardens
8394 McTaggart Street
Mission, British Columbia
V2V 6S6

Gardenimport Inc.
Box 760
Thornhill, Ontario L3T 4A5

Gardens North
34 Helena Street
Ottawa, Ontario K1Y 3M8

Halifax Seed Co. Ltd.
Box 8026, Station A
Halifax, Nova Scotia B3K 5L8

Honeywood Lilies & Nursery
Box 63
Parkside, Saskatchewan S0J 2A0

Hortico Inc.
RR 1
Waterdown, Ontario L0R 2H0

Les Jardins Osiris
838 rue Monique, C.P. 489
St. Thomas, Quebec J0K 3L0

V. Kraus Nurseries Ltd.
Carlisle, Ontario L0R 1H0

Lindenberg Seeds Ltd.
803 Princess Avenue
Brandon, Manitoba R7A 0P5

Miller Bay Farms
248 Wilson Drive
Milton, Ontario L9T 3K2

Monashee Perennials
Site 6, Comp. 9, RR 7
Vernon, British Columbia V1T 7Z3

Morden Nurseries Ltd.
Box 1270
Morden, Manitoba K0G 1J0

McFayden Seed Co. Ltd.
Box 1800
Brandon, Manitoba R7A 6N4

Ontario Seed Co. Ltd.
Box 144
Waterloo, Ontario N2J 3Z9

Parkland Perennials
Box 3683
Spruce Grove, Alberta T7X 3A9

Prism Perennials
Site 25, Comp. 45, RR 1
Castlegar, British Columbia
V1N 3H7

Rainforest Gardens
13139 224th Street, RR 2
Maple Ridge, British Columbia
V2X 7E7

Richters
Box 26
Goodwood, Ontario L0C 1A0

Sherry's Perennials
Box 39
Cedar Springs, Ontario N0P 1E0

Stirling Perennials
RR 1
Morpeth, Ontario N0P 1X0

Stokes Seeds Ltd.
39 James Street, Box 10
St. Catharines, Ontario L2R 6R6

T & T Seeds Ltd.
Box 1710
Winnipeg, Manitoba R3C 3P6

Vesey's Seeds Ltd.
York, Prince Edward Island
C0A 1P0

Woodland Nurseries
2151 Camilla Road
Mississauga, Ontario L5A 2K1

United States

American Daylily & Perennials
Box 7008
The Woodlands, Texas 77387

Cook's Geranium Nursery
712 North Grand
Lyons, Kansas 67554

Cooley's Gardens
11553 Silverton Road N.E.
Silverton, Oregon 97381

Dr. Joseph C. Halinar
2334 Crooked Finger Road
Scotts Mills, Oregon 97375

Johnny's Selected Seeds
299 Foss Hill Road
Albion, Maine 04910

Klehm Nursery
Route 5, Box 197
South Barrington, Illinois 60010

Mellinger's Inc.
2310 W. South Range Road
North Lima, Ohio 44452

Park Seed Co., Inc.
Box 46
Greenwood, South Carolina 29648-0046

Red's Rhodies & Alpine Gardens
15920 S.W. Oberst Lane
Sherwood, Oregon 97140

Redwood City Seed Co.
Box 361
Redwood City, California 94064

Squaw Mountain Gardens
36212 S.E. Squaw Mountain Road
Estacada, Oregon 97023

Sunnybrook Farms Nursery
9448 Mayfield Road, Box 6
Chesterland, Ohio 44026

Thompson & Morgan, Inc.
Box 1308
Jackson, New Jersey 08527

Woodlanders, Inc.
1128 Colleton Avenue
Aiken, South Carolina 29801

Index

94

Credits